WINSTON
CHURCHILL

WORLD LEADERS   PAST AND PRESENT

WINSTON CHURCHILL

Judith Rodgers

HARRAP
London

First published in the United States of America 1986
© 1986 by Chelsea House Publishers
a division of Main Line Book Co.
Introduction © 1985 by Arthur M Schlesinger, jr.
This edition first published in Great Britain 1990
by Harrap Books Ltd
Chelsea House, 26 Market Square,
Bromley, Kent BR1 1NA
New material contained in this edition
© Harrap Books Ltd 1990

All rights reserved. No part of this publication may be reproduced, stored in a retrieval system or transmitted, in any form or by any means, electronic, mechanical, photocopying, recording or otherwise, without the prior permission of Harrap Books Ltd.

ACKNOWLEDGEMENTS
The Author and Publishers are grateful to AP/Wide World Photos, The Bettmann Archive and UPI/Bettmann Newsphotos for their permission to reproduce copyright illustrations in this book.

ISBN 0 245-60098-1 Hardback
ISBN 0 245-60099-X Paperback

Printed in Great Britain by The Bath Press

CONTENTS

On Leadership   7
1. The Hard School of Privilege   13
2. A Soldier's Tale   27
3. In His Father's Footsteps   41
4. The War to End All Wars   51
5. The Uneasy Peace   63
6. The Warlord   73
7. Confronting the Brave New World   95
Further Reading   108
Chronology   109
Index   110

WORLD LEADERS   PAST AND PRESENT

Konrad Adenauer
Alexander the Great
Mark Antony
King Arthur
Kemal Atatürk
Clement Attlee
Menachem Begin
David Ben Gurion
Bismarck
Léon Blum
Símon Bolívar
Cesare Borgia
Willy Brandt
Leonid Brezhnev
Julius Caesar
Calvin
Fidel Castro
Catherine the Great
Charlemagne
Chiang Kai-Shek
Chou En-Lai
Winston Churchill
Clemenceau
Cleopatra
Cortes
Oliver Cromwell
Danton
Charles De Gaulle
De Valera
Disraeli
Dwight D. Eisenhower
Eleanor of Aquitaine
Queen Elizabeth I
Ferdinand and Isabella

Franco
Frederick the Great
Indira Gandhi
Mohandas K. Gandhi
Garibaldi
Genghis Khan
Gladstone
Dag Hammarskjöld
Henry VIII
Henry of Navarre
Hindenburg
Adolf Hitler
Ho Chi Minh
King Hussein
Ivan the Terrible
Andrew Jackson
Thomas Jefferson
Joan of Arc
Pope John XXIII
Lyndon Johnson
Benito Juárez
John F. Kennedy
Jomo Kenyatta
Ayatollah Khomeini
Nikita Khrushchev
Martin Luther King
Henry Kissinger
Vladimir Lenin
Abraham Lincoln
Lloyd George
Louis XIV
Martin Luther
Judas Maccabeus
Mao Tse Tung

Mary, Queen of Scots
Golda Meir
Metternich
Benito Mussolini
Napoleon
Jamal Nasser
Jawalharlal Nehru
Nero
Nicholas II
Richard Nixon
Kwame Nkrumah
Pericles
Juan Perón
Muammar Qaddafi
Robespierre
Eleanor Roosevelt
Franklin D. Roosevelt
Anwar Sadat
Sun Yat-Sen
Joseph Stalin
Tamerlane
Tenzin Gyatso the Dalai Lama
Mother Teresa
Margaret Thatcher
Iosif Tito
Leon Trotsky
Pierre Trudeau
Harry S. Truman
Queen Victoria
George Washington
Chaim Weizmann
Woodrow Wilson
Xerxes

ON LEADERSHIP
Arthur M. Schlesinger, jr.

LEADERSHIP, it may be said, is really what makes the world go round. Love no doubt smooths the passage; but love is a private transaction between consenting adults. Leadership is a public transaction with history. The idea of leadership affirms the capacity of individuals to move, inspire, and mobilize masses of people so that they act together in pursuit of an end. Sometimes leadership serves good purposes, sometimes bad; but whether the end is benign or evil, great leaders are those men and women who leave their personal stamp on history.

Now, the very concept of leadership implies the proposition that individuals can make a difference. This proposition has never been universally accepted. From classical times to the present day, eminent thinkers have regarded individuals as no more than the agents and pawns of larger forces, whether the gods and goddesses of the ancient world or, in the modern era, race, class, nation, the dialectic, the will of the people, the spirit of the times, history itself. Against such forces, the individual dwindles into insignificance.

So contends the thesis of historical determinism. Tolstoy's great novel *War and Peace* offers a famous statement of the case. Why, Tolstoy asked, did millions of men in the Napoleonic Wars, denying their human feelings and their common sense, move back and forth across Europe slaughtering their fellows? "The war," Tolstoy answered, "was bound to happen simply because it was bound to happen." All prior history predetermined it. As for leaders, they, Tolstoy said, "are but the labels that serve to give a name to an end and, like labels, they have the least possible connection with the event." The greater the leader, "the more conspicuous the inevitability and the predestination of every act he commits." The leader, said Tolstoy, is "the slave of history."

Determinism takes many forms. Marxism is the determinism of class. Nazism the determinism of race. But the idea of men and women as the slaves of history runs athwart the deepest human instincts. Rigid determinism abolishes the idea of human freedom—the assumption of free choice that underlies every move we make, every word we speak, every thought we think. It abolishes the idea of human responsibility, since it is manifestly unfair to reward or punish people for actions that are by definition beyond their control. No one can live consistently by any deterministic creed. The Marxist states prove this themselves by their extreme susceptibility to the cult of leadership.

More than that, history refutes the idea that individuals make no difference. In December 1931 a British politician crossing Park Avenue in New York City between 76th and 77th Streets around ten-thirty at night looked in the wrong direction and was knocked down by an automobile—a moment, he later recalled, of a man aghast, a world aglare: "I do not understand why I was not broken like an eggshell or squashed like a gooseberry." Fourteen months later an American politician, sitting in an open car in Miami, Florida, was fired on by an assassin; the man beside him was hit. Those who believe that individuals make no difference to history might well ponder whether the next two decades would have been the same had Mario Constasino's car killed Winston Churchill in 1931 and Giuseppe Zangara's bullet killed Franklin Roosevelt in 1933. Suppose, in addition, that Adolf Hitler had been killed in the street fighting during the Munich *Putsch* of 1923 and that Lenin had died of typhus during World War I. What would the 20th century be like now?

For better or for worse, individuals do make a difference. "The notion that a people can run itself and its affairs anonymously," wrote the philosopher William James, "is now well known to be the silliest of absurdities. Mankind does nothing save through initiatives on the part of inventors, great or small, and imitation by the rest of us—these are the sole factors in human progress. Individuals of genius show the way, and set the patterns, which common people then adopt and follow."

Leadership, James suggests, means leadership in thought as well as in action. In the long run, leaders in thought may well make the greater difference to the world. But, as Woodrow Wilson once said, "Those only are leaders of men, in the general eye, who lead in action. . . . It is at their hands that new thought gets its translation into the crude language of deeds." Leaders in thought often invent in solitude and obscurity, leaving to later generations the tasks of imitation. Leaders in action—the leaders portrayed in this series—have to be effective in their own time.

And they cannot be effective by themselves. They must act in response to the rhythms of their age. Their genius must be adapted, in a phrase of William James's, "to the receptivities of the moment." Leaders are useless without followers. "There goes the mob," said the French politician hearing a clamour in the streets. "I am their leader. I must follow them." Great leaders turn the inchoate emotions of the mob to purposes of their own.

They seize on the opportunities of their time, the hopes, fears, frustrations, crises, potentialities. They succeed when events have prepared the way for them, when the community is awaiting to be aroused, when they can provide the clarifying and organizing ideas. Leadership ignites the circuit between the individual and the mass and thereby alters history.

It may alter history for better or for worse. Leaders have been responsible for the most extravagant follies and most monstrous crimes that have beset suffering humanity. They have also been vital in such gains as humanity has made in individual freedom, religious and racial tolerance, social justice, and respect for human rights.

There is no sure way to tell in advance who is going to lead for good and who for evil. But a glance at the gallery of men and women in *World Leaders—Past and Present* suggests some useful tests.

One test is this: Do leaders lead by force or by persuasion? By command or by consent? Through most of history leadership was exercised by the divine right of authority. The duty of followers was to defer and to obey. "Theirs not to reason why / Theirs but to do and die." On occasion, as with the so-called enlightened despots of the 18th century in Europe, absolutist leadership was animated by humane purposes. More often, absolutism nourished the passion for domination, land, gold, and conquest and resulted in tyranny.

The great revolution of modern times has been the revolution of equality. The idea that all people should be equal in their legal condition has undermined the old structure of authority, hierarchy, and deference. The revolution of equality has had two contrary effects on the nature of leadership. For equality, as Alexis de Tocqueville pointed out in his great study *Democracy in America,* might mean equality in servitude as well as equality in freedom.

"I know of only two methods of establishing equality in the political world," Tocqueville wrote. "Rights must be given to every citizen, or none at all to anyone . . . save one, who is the master of all." There was no middle ground "between the sovereignty of all and the absolute power of one man." In his astonishing prediction of 20th-century totalitarian dictatorship, Tocqueville explained how the revolution of equality could lead to the *"Führerprinzip"* and more terrible absolutism than the world had ever known.

But when rights are given to every citizen and the sovereignty of all is established, the problem of leadership takes a new form, becomes more exacting than ever before. It is easy to issue commands and enforce them by the rope and the stake, the concentration camp and the *gulag.* It is much harder to use argument and achievement to overcome opposition and win consent. The Founding Fathers of the United States understood the difficulty. They believed that history had given them the opportunity to decide, as Alexander Hamilton wrote in the first Federalist Paper, whether men are indeed capable of basing government on "reflection and choice, or whether they are forever destined to depend . . . on accident and force."

Government by reflection and choice called for a new style of leadership and a new quality of followership. It required leaders to be responsive to popular concerns, and it required followers to be active and informed participants in the process. Democracy does not eliminate emotion from politics; sometimes it fosters demagoguery; but it is confident that, as the greatest of democratic leaders put it, you cannot fool all of the people all of the time. It measures leadership by results and retires those who overreach or falter or fail.

It is true that in the long run despots are measured by results too. But they can postpone the day of judgment, sometimes indefinitely, and in the meantime they can do infinite harm. It is also true that democracy is no guarantee of virtue and intelligence in government, for the voice of the people is not necessarily the voice of God. But democracy, by assuring the right of opposition, offers built-in resistance to the evils inherent in absolutism. As the theologian Reinhold Niebuhr summed it up, "Man's capacity for justice makes democracy possible, but man's inclination to injustice makes democracy necessary."

A second test for leadership is the end for which power is sought. When leaders have as their goal the supremacy of a master race or the promotion of totalitarian revolution or the acquisition and exploitation of colonies or the protection of greed and privilege or the preservation of personal power, it is likely that their leadership will do little to advance the cause of humanity. When their goal is the abolition of slavery, the liberation of women, the enlargement of opportunity for the poor and powerless, the extension of equal rights to racial minorities, the defence of the freedoms of expression and opposition, it is likely that their leadership will increase the sum of human liberty and welfare.

Leaders have done great harm to the world. They have also conferred great benefits. You will find both sorts in this series. Even "good" leaders must be regarded with a certain wariness.

Leaders are not demigods; they put on their trousers one leg after another just like ordinary mortals. No leader is infallible, and every leader needs to be reminded of this at regular intervals. Irreverence irritates leaders but is their salvation. Unquestioning submission corrupts leaders and demeans followers. Making a cult of a leader is always a mistake. Fortunately hero worship generates its own antidote. "Every hero," said Emerson, "becomes a bore at last."

The signal benefit the great leaders confer is to embolden the rest of us to live according to our own best selves, to be active, insistent, and resolute in affirming our own sense of things. For great leaders attest to the reality of human freedom against the supposed inevitabilities of history. And they attest to the wisdom and power that may lie within the most unlikely of us, which is why Abraham Lincoln remains the supreme example of great leadership. A great leader, said Emerson, exhibits new possibilities to all humanity. "We feed on genius. . . . Great men exist that there may be greater men."

Great leaders, in short, justify themselves by emancipating and empowering their followers. So humanity struggles to master its destiny, remembering with Alexis de Tocqueville: "It is true that around every man a fatal circle is traced beyond which he cannot pass; but within the wide verge of that circle he is powerful and free; as it is with man, so with communities."

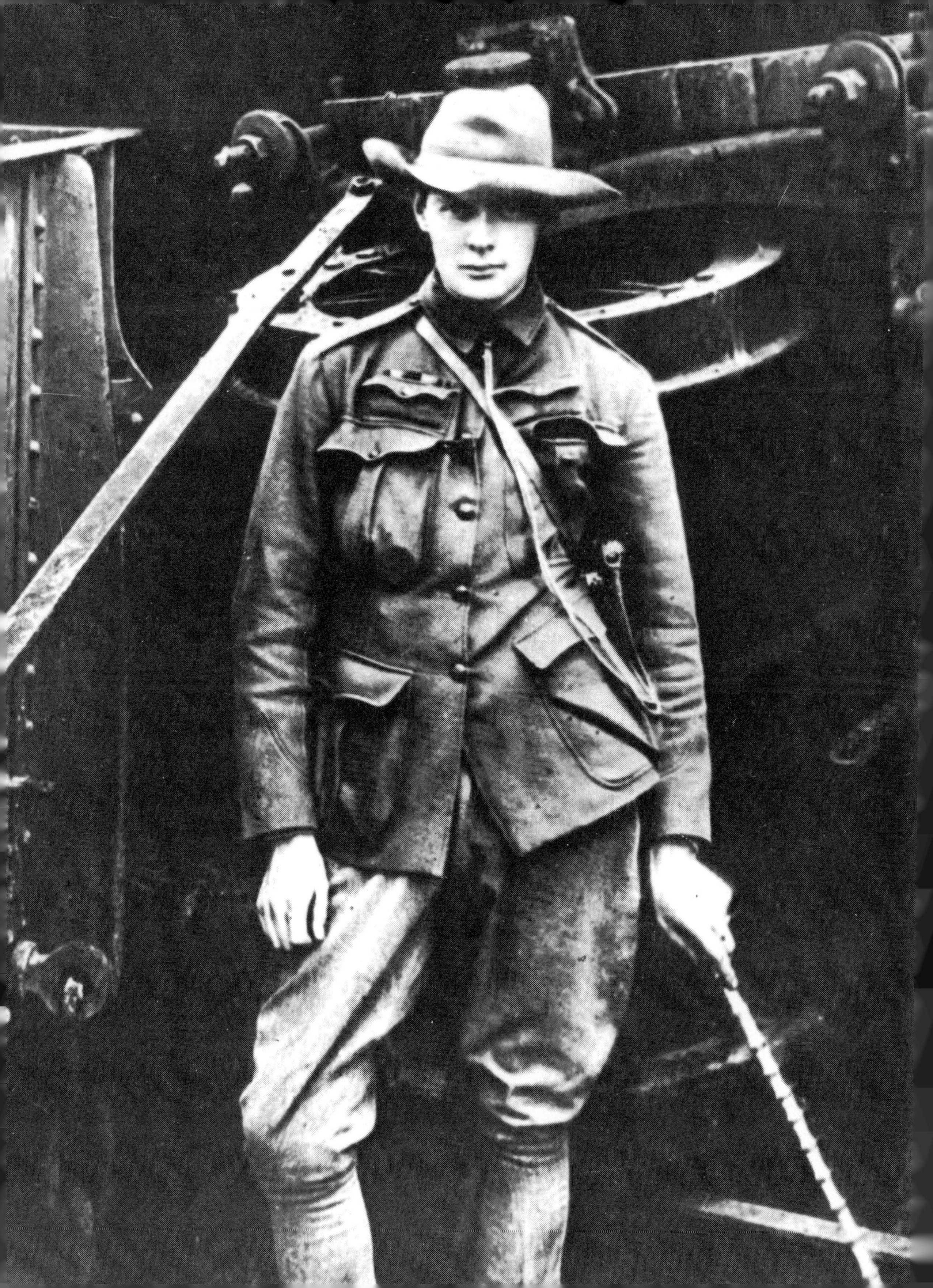

1
The Hard School of Privilege

> *He is always unconsciously playing a part—an heroic part. And he is himself the most astonished spectator. He sees himself moving through the smoke of battle—triumphant, terrible, his brow clothed with thunder, his legions looking to him for victory, and not looking in vain.*
> —A. G. GARDINER
> British journalist

As a young newspaper correspondent in 1899, Winston Churchill was sent by the London *Morning Post* to cover the Boer War in South Africa. Like most soldiers and officers he met there, Winston anticipated an easy British victory. But the Boers, the people of Dutch, German, and Huguenot ancestry who had settled in South Africa over 200 years earlier, proved to be fierce and determined fighters. In fact, within a month after war had been declared, they had taken the offensive. (The original cause of the dispute was the Boers' refusal to grant civil rights to the many British citizens who had come to seek their fortunes in the gold fields of the Boer republics of Transvaal and the Orange Free State.)

Shortly after he arrived, Winston joined the British military on a dangerous mission to patrol enemy lines. Their armoured train was ambushed on the way to the front. He and 57 others were taken prisoner and brought to Pretoria, the enemy capital.

One night about a month later, in a daring move, Churchill managed to scramble over the prison wall to freedom. It was an extremely bold and risky venture, as he certainly would have been shot had

War correspondent Winston Churchill (1874–1965) prepares to board an armoured train heading towards the Boer lines in 1899. He was, he later wrote, "eager for trouble."

Young Winston sports his sailor suit, a popular costume among boys of his time. Until he was sent away to school at the age of seven, Winston spent most of his time with his beloved nanny, Elizabeth Everest, or in solitary games with his huge collection of toy soldiers.

13

Churchill expected to find either Boers or hostile native warriors when he wearily approached the lights of a settlement after his dramatic escape from prison. When the inhabitants of the first house he came to proved to be British, he felt, he said later, "like a drowning man pulled out of the water and informed he has won the Derby."

he been detected. Once outside the detention centre he still faced numerous obstacles. He was 300 miles west of a friendly border, without food, and with no map or compass to guide him. And surely his captors would soon be in pursuit. The exit routes from town were patrolled by the enemy, and all trains were being carefully searched. To complicate matters even further, he could not speak Afrikaans, the Dutch-derived language of the Boers.

Yet Churchill was confident. Somehow, he would find a way out of his predicament. After making his way to the outskirts of Pretoria, he eventually reached a railway track. Having walked along the track for about two hours, he finally spotted a railway station ahead. He decided to hide on the first train that came by, although he was unsure whether it would be taking him eastward towards freedom. He calculated that if he walked past the station and hid in the bush just beyond the boarding platform, he might be able to jump onto the train as it departed.

About an hour later he heard the whistle of an approaching train. He waited nervously as the freight train stopped at the station. As it pulled away heading toward him, he realized it was going faster than he had expected. Suddenly flashing lights were upon him, the huge locomotive directly above, pouring forth clouds of steam. He hurled himself at one of the passing cars, grasping at anything to latch onto. With a struggle he was able to pull himself aboard. Exhausted, he nestled among the sacks of goods and was soon fast asleep. By morning he knew he must leave the train or risk being caught. He jumped off, and watched the train disappear into the rising sun, pleased that at least he had been carried eastward.

He set off for the hills to find a place to hide, trudging doggedly onward in the sweltering heat. He could see a native village and a few enemy soldiers, and knew what it felt like to be a wanted man. He had to escape from the country at once.

In spite of the danger, he was charged with eagerness; at the age of 25, Churchill was filled with a spirit of adventure. Trained as a soldier, he had already fought in three wars—in Cuba, India, and along the Nile—but had left the army a year before to begin a career in politics. He had lost his first run for office, and when the Boer War broke out, he

Well-armed and confident, Boer militiamen relax between battles. Correspondent Churchill conceded that the Boers were "brave," but he also referred to them as a "savage tribe" whose behaviour was "gross, fierce, and horrid."

By the end of the 19th century British financier Cecil Rhodes (seated, fourth from left, 1853–1902) had made himself the most powerful man in Africa and one of the richest in the world.

had wanted to be in on the action, and was certainly seeing some now.

At this point, there seemed only one way out: to board a freight train as it began its slow chug up through the hills. He planned to repeat the previous night's tactic—ride the train under cover of darkness and then jump off just before daybreak. If he did this three nights in a row, Churchill figured, he would be out of enemy territory.

He waited far into the night but no train came. In the moonlight he walked until he reached a station, where three freight trains stood, motionless. He could hide in one of them until morning, and stay on board until it reached its final stop. He did not know, however, where the trains were going. He crept up to a car to look for markings of some kind. Suddenly he heard loud voices, speaking Afrikaans, coming toward the train from the other side. He fled into the night and out onto the open plain.

Exhausted as he was, he had no choice but to keep walking. He was utterly alone in the darkness, and the few houses visible were strictly off limits. Suddenly he noticed a row of bright lights on the horizon. As he came closer to the distant lights he saw that they illuminated not a native encampment, but several stone houses clustered around a coal mine.

Was this his chance, he wondered. He realized that if he continued on alone, not knowing where he was going, he would either be caught or forced to give himself up rather than starve. Winston had heard that a few British mining experts had been allowed to stay in this district and he sincerely hoped that the home in front of him housed an ally. Despite knowing that the odds were against him, he walked to the door and knocked loudly.

"Who is it?" a voice answered in Afrikaans, and Churchill was stricken with disappointment.

"I need help. I have had an accident," he heard himself say.

The front door opened and a tall man stood before him. "What do you want?" he asked, in English.

Churchill told the man he was a merchant and that he had fallen from a train and was hurt. The man looked at him, then ushered him into the house. Churchill sat down at a table and waited for the man to speak.

"I'd like to know a little more about this accident of yours," he said.

Churchill swallowed hard. "I think I'd better tell you the truth."

"I think you had," the man said.

"I am Winston Churchill, war correspondent for the London *Morning Post*. I escaped last night from Pretoria. I am making my way to the frontier. Will you help me?"

A long, ominous silence followed. Finally, the man got up and locked the door. "Thank God you have come here!" he said. "It is the only house in 20 miles where you would not have been handed over. But we are all British here and we will see you through."

Churchill had never felt such relief. The man introduced himself as Mr. Howard, manager of the local mine and one of only four Englishmen in the entire area. He warned Churchill that the authorities had been around earlier that day looking for him. By harbouring a wanted man, Mr. Howard was placing himself in danger.

"We will think of a plan for your escape," he said. "But until then I must hide you." Mr. Howard took Churchill out into the night, towards the entrance to the mineshaft. They went down into the darkness.

Churchill remained in the rat-infested mine for

> *His playroom contained from one end to the other a plank table on trestles, upon which were thousands of lead soldiers arranged for battle. He organized wars. The lead battalions were manoeuvred into action, peas and pebbles committed great casualties, forts were stormed, cavalry charged, real water-tanks engulfed the advancing foe.*
> —CLARE SHERIDAN
> a cousin of Winston Churchill

Jennie Churchill embraces her first child, Winston. Remarks about his having arrived only seven months after his parents' marriage followed Churchill all his life, but he never took them seriously. "Although present on the occasion," he once said of his birth, "I have no clear recollection of the events leading up to it."

three days. On the fourth day Mr. Howard came with an escape plan. In three days there was to be a shipment of wool bound for Portuguese East Africa (now Mozambique) loaded aboard a train at the rail station that served the mine. With luck, Churchill could be concealed among the bales packed into the car. Since the freight car would be covered with a heavy, tightly sealed canvas, there was a good chance that the contents of the car would not be too carefully checked at the border. Howard then asked Churchill if he was willing to take such a risk.

Despite the obvious dangers, Churchill agreed. At 2:00 A.M. on December 19, 1899, Mr. Howard silently led Churchill to the loading area, where he hoisted himself into the freight car and squeezed into an opening between the bales, worming his way to the centre. At daybreak the long trip began.

He had memorized the names of all the stations along the line and had hoped to count them off through a tiny crack in the cargo as the hours passed. But he could see very little. He sat still, afraid to move, for at more than one station he heard Boer voices only a few feet away.

Finally, at 11:00 P.M. that night, the train pulled to a stop and Churchill glimpsed a sign bearing a Portuguese place name. At last he was out of enemy territory. He scrambled to the rear of the car, pushed his head outside, and fired his revolver several times, overjoyed at his success.

News of Churchill's escape soon reached the press, and when he arrived in Durban, the major seaport of the British colony of Natal, he received a hero's welcome and was praised for his courage and daring.

Churchill's bold enterprise brought him the fame and glory he had dreamed of, and projected him into the public eye, where he would remain for the rest of his life. Within months he was elected to Parliament. He went on to serve more than 50 years in public office, holding posts both military and civilian, supervising domestic and overseas affairs and ultimately becoming England's greatest leader in adversity during World War II.

The same determination that Winston Churchill demonstrated in his escape from the Boers served him throughout his long career. His was a career touched by failure as well as glory: for example, Churchill was held responsible for the disastrous defeat the British suffered at Gallipoli in Turkey during World War I. But no matter how great the odds, nothing could stop him from serving his country and pursuing his personal ambitions. When all hope seemed lost, Churchill often shone. He became prime minister in 1940, when things seemed bleakest, and led Great Britain through its darkest hour. By inspiring his people with his brilliant speeches, Churchill rallied his country to its valiant triumph in the Battle of Britain. Though far outnumbered, the Royal Air Force defeated Hitler's air raiders, the *Luftwaffe*. And Churchill, working with American President Franklin D. Roosevelt and Soviet leader Joseph Stalin, helped produce an Allied victory in 1945.

Churchill's parents, however, had believed that hope for young Winston had been lost from the start. He hated to study, overspent his allowance, and did poorly in school. His father, Lord Randolph Churchill, a Member of Parliament, was sure his son would not amount to much—he certainly would not get into the university. A military career was the best Winston could hope for, thought Randolph. (Churchill had to take the entrance examinations for the military academy three times before he passed.) But in fact Winston was doing his own kind of studying. He watched people closely, enemies as well as friends, and considered all sides of an issue. And as a young soldier in India he made up for lost time by reading volumes of history and biographies of world leaders—as if in preparation for the role he would later play.

Though his father thought otherwise, Winston never believed that he would stay in the military for long. He considered it a stepping-stone to a political career. He knew what he wanted and would do whatever it took to get it. During his childhood he confidently told people that he would one day be a statesman like his father. As a young man he

Lord Randolph Churchill (1849–1895) in 1889. Seriously ill by this time, "Lord Randy" still seemed a commanding figure to his son, who worshipped him. Churchill later wrote that his father seemed "to own the key to everything or almost everything worth having."

was so ambitious, proud, and outspoken that many people accused him of being nothing but a glory-hunter.

Churchill was courageous, and willing to go it alone. He never feared the prospect of battle, and he never ceased to prepare himself for conflicts that he considered inevitable. In the early 1930s, when many thought him misguided, Churchill was almost alone in speaking out against Hitler. And in World War II his "V for victory" signal became a symbol of enduring faith in the justice of the British cause.

When Churchill died in 1965 at the age of 90, he received a state funeral as glorious as any in English history. He died a nobleman, having been knighted by the queen in 1953. That same year, he had won the Nobel Prize for Literature, the highest honour accorded to writers. Throughout his remarkable life Churchill was often able to accomplish things quite beyond most people's capabilities. It is clear that he conducted his life—and his career—in keeping with one piece of advice he gave himself and others: "Never, never, never give in."

Winston Leonard Spencer Churchill was born on November 30, 1874, at Blenheim Palace, the huge country mansion owned by his grandparents, the duke and duchess of Marlborough. His parents were visiting the estate from their home in London when Winston arrived.

Winston was the first child born to Jennie and Randolph Churchill, who had been married earlier that year. Randolph was an aristocrat, a member of England's upper class. The Churchills were one of the old, landowning families of Britain. There had been a long line of dukes in Randolph's family, and his father had been a Member of Parliament, the nation's governing body. Jennie was an heiress, the daughter of Leonard Jerome, an American businessman who had made a fortune on Wall Street.

In spite of the wealth that both Randolph and Jennie enjoyed, their marriage was beset with difficulties from the start. Jennie was an unusually beautiful young socialite when she met Randolph. He was twenty-five, five years older than she, and about to embark upon a career in politics. They fell in love immediately and became engaged a short time later. His parents, however, objected—his father wanted to know more about the Jerome family first. In those days it was rare for a Briton, especially one from an aristocratic family like Randolph's, to marry an American, even a rich heiress. Jennie's father was also unhappy about the match. Leonard Jerome had made his own fortune and did not think much of the British aristocracy whose members had merely inherited their wealth. Grudgingly, he gave his consent, but it took Randolph months to persuade his own parents to agree. Even then, they refused to attend the wedding.

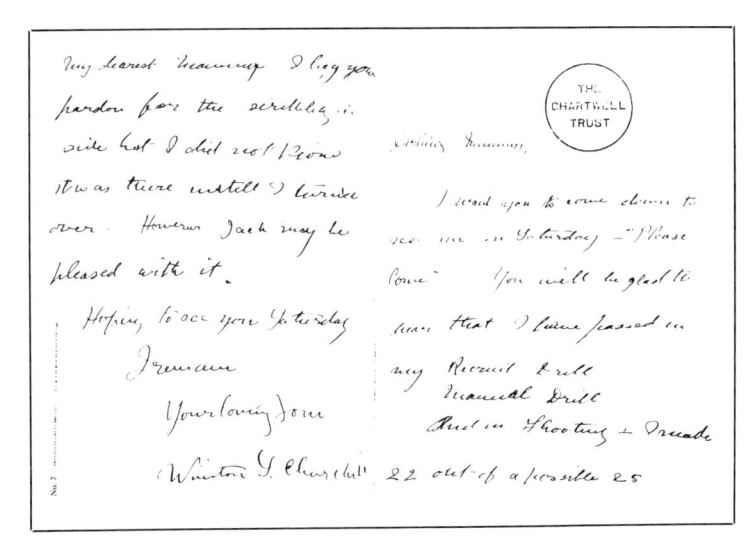

When Jennie became pregnant, she withdrew from society for several months, as was the custom among women of the class into which she had married. Generally much sought after and constantly to be seen at parties, she did not much like the idea of confinement. So when Winston was only a few weeks old, he was handed over to a nurse. Later a nanny would take on the job of caring for him throughout his childhood years. Jennie returned to the duties and pleasures of life in high society and paid her son occasional visits.

Winston was barely three months old when his father fell ill. Randolph's health began to deteriorate, and continued to do so for the next 20 years.

Writing from school ("Darling Mummy, I want you to come down to see me. . . . Please come . . . "), Winston accidentally used a sheet of paper on which he had sketched battle scenes. Fearful of offending his mother, Jennie Churchill (1854–1921), he added, "I beg your pardon for the scribbling."

His illness prevented him from being a strong father to Winston and from achieving the greatness for which many of his contemporaries had thought him destined.

Winston's parents, therefore, were distant figures who never gave him much love. They came to see him only occasionally. And yet, in an uncritical, almost worshipful way, he adored them.

When Winston was five, his brother Jack was born. The two boys were very different, in looks and in disposition—Jack was quiet and easygoing while Winston was extremely boisterous.

Because their parents were so active and seldom together, the boys had little real home life. Winston spent most of his time with Mrs. Everest, his kind and loving nanny, who gave him the care his parents never did. During his early childhood he often travelled with Jack and Mrs. Everest to Blenheim Palace or to the seaside. When Winston was seven his parents sent him to St. George's, a school designed to prepare young boys for public school.

Winston hated St. George's, did poorly in his studies, and received nothing but bad reports. He would write to his parents, asking them to visit him, but they would not even answer his letters. At St. George's, Winston was always in some kind of trouble. The punishment for bad behaviour was a flogging by the headmaster. The floggings were very

Jack Churchill (left; 1880–1947), poses with his mother and his older brother, Winston. The boys were as unlike as two people can be: Jack was quiet and obedient; Winston was, as one of his schoolmasters put it, "a constant trouble to everybody and ... always in some scrape or other."

severe and painful, and when Winston came home from St. George's with welts, he was removed from the school. In September 1884 Winston was transferred to a school in Brighton. There his work improved, but his behaviour did not. His experiences at St. George's had made him determined not to be bullied by anyone.

By this time, Winston's father had become a man of considerable prominence. He too was gaining a reputation for independence and directness. In 1885 he became secretary of state for India, which was then part of the British Empire. A few months later, in 1886, he was appointed Chancellor of the Exchequer, in charge of the British economy. At the same time he was also leader of the House of Commons. Winston was proud of his father and asked him to send autographs for his classmates.

At the age of 37, however, Randolph looked and acted like a sick and feeble old man. As his illness got worse, he became increasingly bad-tempered and liable to quarrel without provocation. Randolph was clearly less suitable than he had been for the responsible and demanding positions he held. He resigned as chancellor after only six months. He became very intolerant of Winston's failings, and he would go into a rage whenever confronted with bad school reports.

By 1888 Winston was in his last year at Brighton and ready to move on to public school. Apart from his poor grades in Latin, he had been a fair student overall. His parents decided that he should go to Harrow. When the time for the Harrow entrance examination came, Winston managed to scrape by despite the fact that he had become so nervous in the Latin portion that he failed to answer a single question. He graduated from Brighton at the bottom of his class.

Pupils at Harrow received a traditional education. Students had to concentrate especially hard on Latin and Greek, and were also required to gain some grounding in the natural sciences and mathematics. Boys intended for military careers attended army class, which at Harrow was considered less than prestigious.

> *He consistently broke almost every rule made by masters or boys, was quite incorrigible, and had an unlimited vocabulary of 'backchat' which he produced with dauntless courage on every occasion of remonstrance.*
> —SIR GERALD WOODS WOLLASTON
> schoolmate of Churchill's at Harrow

> [Churchill] was blessed with length of days, and he came to the supreme achievement of his life schooled and disciplined by long experience of great affairs, familiar with the handling and control of national problems, full of practical wisdom, and with a part to play that he alone could most magnificently fulfill.
> —LORD JUSTICE BIRKETT

During his first year at Harrow, Winston's work was fair, but his conduct was poor; he was careless, forgetful, and often late. His lack of application greatly disturbed his parents. What Jennie and Randolph thought, however, did not seem to concern Winston, who continued to get into scrapes and ask for money. He was even put "on report," which meant that his work was watched closely by the headmaster. He hated it and begged his mother to do something.

Randolph, who was always ready to believe the worst about Winston, was completely disgusted with him. Convinced that Winston would never get into Oxford or Cambridge, England's most prestigious universities, Randolph asked his son if he would like to go into the army.

Winston jumped at the chance, excited by the possibility of leading troops into battle. He loved everything military and had 1,500 toy soldiers with which he played constantly. Randolph had him transferred to the army class.

Besides his bad grades Winston's frequent requests for money constantly upset his parents. His father angrily compared him to his brother Jack, who was always at the top of his class at Brighton. His mother pleaded with him to study hard and do his absolute best to pass the first examination for the Royal Military Academy at Sandhurst.

When Winston did apply himself, he did quite well. In 1890 he managed to pass the preliminary test, which satisfied his parents for the time being. Even though they thought he would never make much of his life, Winston remained supremely self-confident. He also impressed other adults who met him.

One person that Winston managed to charm was the doctor he visited soon after passing his examination. The doctor was a famous specialist in London (he treated the royal family), and Winston went to see him for the correction of a lisp.

"But that cannot matter so very much," the doctor said. "It will not interfere with you in the army."

"You do not understand," said Winston. "Of course I intend to go to Sandhurst and join a regiment in

India. But I am going to become a statesman like my father, and when I do, I must be able to make an important speech without worrying that I cannot say the letter s."

When the thin, red-haired boy left, the doctor went in to see his wife. "I've just seen the most extraordinary young man I have ever met." Winston was 16 years old.

Instead of studying and preparing for his Sandhurst final examination, Winston enjoyed his last years at Harrow by fencing and writing controversial articles for the school newspaper. Even though he had had a private tutor, he failed the examination badly. His parents were furious, and Randolph, now very ill indeed, was certain his son would end up in a clerk's job. When Winston failed the examination again a few months later, his father was not surprised. By this time, even Winston felt low. He had no choice but to go to a special "cram" class to prepare for the test. It was said that only born idiots failed the examinations after cramming, and Winston finally came through in June 1893, on his third try.

Winston was thrilled that he had finally done what his father had wanted him to do. But Randolph was far from happy, since Winston had failed to make the grade for an infantry cadetship and would have to join the cavalry—a less prestigious fighting arm. He told Winston that he considered his performance unacceptable. In his father's eyes, Winston was still a failure.

Yet Winston did not lose confidence. Even though there was nothing he could do to satisfy his father, he did want to please him, and promised to do better at Sandhurst.

Although his father showed him very little affection and spoke only of Winston's failures, Winston's relationship with his father was a major shaping force in his life. Winston never ceased in his attempts to win his father's approval. Rather than see Randolph for what he was—a once-great man now well past the peak of his powers—Winston idolized his father and saw him as an important and influential statesman.

As a student at Harrow School, Winston Churchill looked like the perfect young Victorian gentleman, but his behaviour was unimproved. Angered by his endless "backchat," the headmaster once snapped, "Churchill, I have grave reason to be displeased with you." Winston quickly responded: "And I, sir, have grave reason to be displeased with you."

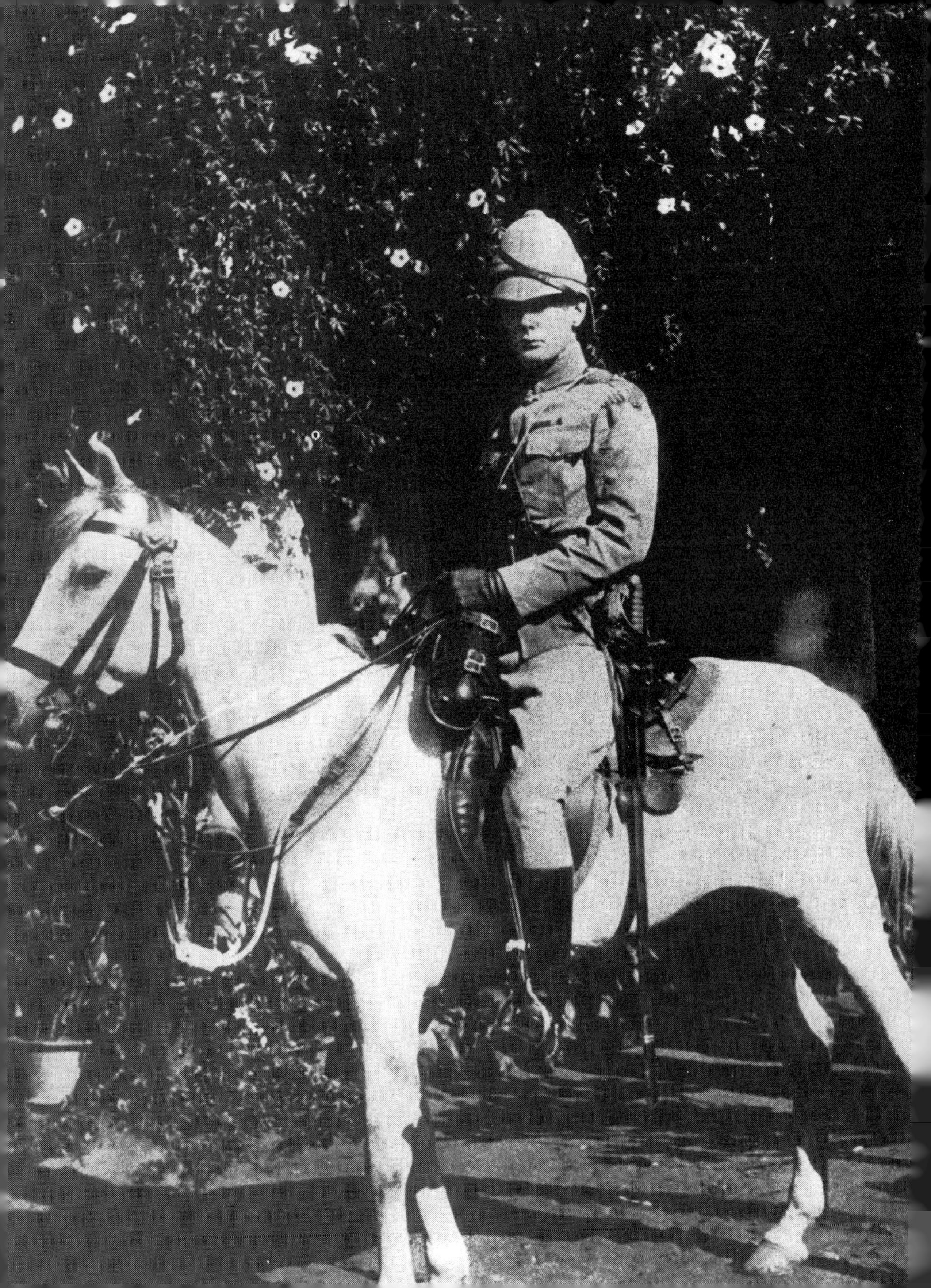

2
A Soldier's Tale

> *It is better to be making the news than taking it; to be an actor than a critic.*
> —WINSTON CHURCHILL

On September 1, 1893, 18-year-old Winston Churchill arrived at the Royal Military Academy. He was one of 120 "gentleman cadets" in the entering class who would spend their next year and a half being trained as infantry officers. (Churchill had finally gained an infantry cadetship because boys with higher marks than his had decided to pursue other careers, which meant that the army command had to increase admissions of infantry cadets by transferring cavalry cadets like Winston.)

Sandhurst was very different from any other school Winston had attended. The curriculum consisted of riding, drill, manoeuvres, and the study of such subjects as tactics, fortification, and military law. Discipline was very strict. Winston was learning the routines and rituals of military life, from keeping accounts for a regiment to conducting an inspection. For once he loved his schoolwork.

Winston knew that his career would depend on his performance at Sandhurst, and he applied himself eagerly. It was not easy for him, and the physical training especially was rigorous for the short, skinny cadet. For the first time he pushed himself to excel.

In 1895, shortly after his father's death, Churchill donned the resplendent, scarlet-and-gold uniform of the Fourth Hussars. His acceptance into the exclusive cavalry regiment was arranged by his mother, who had finally taken an interest in her adoring son. "Indeed," he later wrote, "she soon became an ardent ally."

Like the other men of the Fourth Hussars, Churchill had little to do but exercise fast horses and quick wit. Accosted by a woman who told him she disliked both his politics and his new moustache, the young officer declared, "Madam, I see no earthly reason why you should come into contact with either."

Churchill's first book, which appeared in 1898, sold 8,500 copies and earned him more money than four years' salary in the army. The warm reception of *The Story of the Malakand Field Force*, which was hailed as a minor classic, filled its 23-year-old author with "pride and pleasure." He had, he noted, "never been praised before."

THE STORY

OF THE

MALAKAND FIELD FORCE

AN EPISODE OF FRONTIER WAR

BY

WINSTON L. SPENCER CHURCHILL
Lieutenant, the 4th Queen's Own Hussars

"They (Frontier Wars) are but the surf that marks the edge and the advance of the wave of civilisation."
LORD SALISBURY, Guildhall, 1892

WITH MAPS, PLANS, ETC.

LONGMANS, GREEN, AND CO.
39 PATERNOSTER ROW, LONDON
NEW YORK AND BOMBAY
1898

Winston was happy at Sandhurst, and the effects showed. Randolph approved of Winston's neat appearance and good manners and began introducing him to political leaders and young men on the rise in politics. Winston was thrilled with these new opportunities, but whenever he looked to Randolph for love and friendship, his father was always cold and disapproving. Randolph still seemed to derive much pleasure from finding fault with his son. Yet when his father attacked him unfairly or compared him to Jack, Winston would apologize rather than defend himself.

Winston was becoming a man, and one of his responsibilities was having patience with his dying father. Randolph's condition had deteriorated to the point of madness. Unfortunately, he insisted on attending sessions of Parliament, where he embarrassed others pitifully. The man whose brilliant speeches had once greatly moved that august assembly now spoke in a disconnected, almost delirious manner. When Randolph got up to speak, others would stand to leave.

In 1894 Randolph's doctors finally persuaded him to go on a long sea voyage for the sake of his health and state of mind. Jennie agreed to accompany him, and they sailed on June 27.

With his parents away, Winston was free to manage his own affairs. Having become an excellent rider at Sandhurst, he now decided that he wished to join a cavalry regiment after all. He was enjoying himself, spending more money than he had, writing happy letters to his father about his everyday life. But it was Jennie who wrote back, and her tone was strange and frightening. Winston called the family doctor, who told him the truth about Randolph's condition.

Though the news was a painful shock to Winston, he did not let it distract him from his studies at Sandhurst. At long last, Winston could declare himself an academic success. In December 1894 he graduated in the top 15 percent of his class.

Randolph and Jennie arrived back in London on Christmas Eve. The trip had proved too much for a man in Randolph's condition, and the doctors said that he now had but days to live. Winston had hoped that his father would be pleased with his good grades, but Randolph was slipping in and out of a coma, and could hardly recognize his son. Finally, on January 24, 1895, Randolph died painlessly in his sleep.

Despite Winston's immediate and natural sense of loss, Randolph's death actually marked the beginning of an exciting new stage in his life. No longer would he have to suffer his father's negative judgments and try in vain to prove himself. Winston had often dreamed of joining his father in politics, and Randolph's death did not diminish his desire to enter public life. Now he began to calculate how best he might get himself elected. To Winston, gaining fame and prominence for military exploits seemed the best way of coming to the voters' attention.

Horatio Herbert Kitchener (1850–1916), the general whose activities were criticized by Churchill in 1898, was one of England's most popular heroes. After Omdurman, he fought in the Boer War, served as commander in chief in India, proconsul of Egypt, secretary of war, and, finally, organizer of British forces in World War I.

Gold miners in the Boer Republic of Transvaal. Like most Englishmen, Churchill felt that all Africa should be British. "Sooner or later," he wrote, "for the sake of our Empire, for the sake of our honour, for the sake of the race, we must fight the Boers."

He was now ready to enter the army, and he joined a cavalry regiment stationed about 35 miles from London. The training was difficult, and he put in long hours. But there was plenty of time left over for socializing and for playing polo, at which he became quite skilled.

Since Churchill considered a career in the army his only possible passport to fame, he began to wish for some real action. In 1895, however, there was war in only one spot on the globe—and it was not a British affair. In Cuba rebels were fighting for their independence from Spain. Churchill, who had 10 weeks leave from his regiment at that time, began to pull the necessary strings. After obtaining a letter of introduction from the Spanish authorities via Britain's ambassador in Madrid (an old friend of his father's), he went straight to the War Office to get official British permission.

Delighted by his acceptance, Churchill proposed the idea that he would write newspaper reports about the war to pay his way. The London *Daily Graphic* agreed, and offered him a fee for every article he wrote.

Churchill arrived in Havana, Cuba, on November 20. With his letter of introduction, he was received by the Spanish general at the front. He received his baptism of fire on December 1, when the unit to which he was attached came under attack from Cuban rebels. In his first battle, he won a medal for gallantry.

During his six weeks in Cuba, Churchill gained considerable public attention—and much of it was negative. The newspapers frowned on his "visiting" the scene of a war in which Britain was not involved. Despite this controversy, Churchill had proved himself to be an excellent field journalist. His reports took account of both sides of the dispute and demonstrated much insight into the issues at stake.

On his return to London, Churchill turned his attention to other matters. Always trying to advance himself, he began to make use of the political connections he had made through his father. Though he was only 21, Churchill was at home with the political leaders of his day, and expressed his opinions freely. He began to think of himself as someone important, and was impatient to place himself in politics, where he could make a difference.

However, the young Churchill knew that first he would have to make his mark in the army, to gain a name for himself by winning medals and becoming famous through battle. Besides, the army was his only source of income, and money was an important concern for a young man starting out in politics. In those days Members of Parliament received no salary.

Still, the fame and glory that Churchill considered essential to political advancement seemed nowhere in sight in the context of the military. His regiment was due to leave for India, which at that time offered no prospect of battle whatsoever. He tried to get a transfer and failed.

In October of 1896, he and his fellow soldiers arrived in Bombay, India. From there, they made their way to the south, where they were stationed.

The life of a peacetime British army officer in India was luxurious. There was little for Churchill to do but play polo, and his regiment soon became one of the best of all those stationed in India.

It did not take long for Churchill to become bored. The thought of being an idle soldier was more than he could stand. He made up his mind that he would spend his free hours reading, and thus improve his education. For four or five hours a day,

Queen Victoria (1819–1901) reigned for 64 years and gave her name to an era. Sovereign of a quarter of the earth, she was regarded as divine by many of her subjects, who comprised more than a quarter of the world's population. She was displeased by Churchill's reports of the atrocities that Kitchener had sanctioned against tribesmen in the Sudan in 1898.

while the other officers played cards, he read history and philosophy. Nothing he read was lost on him, for he had an excellent memory. The knowledge he acquired turned out to be of great value for it helped to enlarge his understanding of human events and to expand the range of his writing.

After being stationed in India for eight months, he received three months' leave, and decided to return to Britain for the summer, setting himself the goal of political advancement. His best chance, he believed, would be in the Conservative party, the party to which his father had belonged. He persisted until he got what he wanted—the chance to make his first public speech.

On July 26, 1897, he spoke in the ancient town of Bath. The crowd cheered him loudly, and the newspapers gave him good reviews.

A few days later, he was greatly interested to read news of a frontier war in India. Native tribesmen in the strategically important Swat Valley, near India's northern border, had rebelled against the British, who were endeavouring to civilize and militarize the area. Churchill could not get a post with the three brigades selected to crush the uprising. When the commander of the field force suggested that he join the expedition as a reporter, he managed to get a contract from the London *Daily Telegraph.* He was thrilled to be going to the scene of action once again.

During his six weeks at the frontier, Churchill sent 15 letters to the *Daily Telegraph* describing the strange war against the tribesmen. He also saw his first proper active service in a series of engagements that were very costly to the British, who lost 150 men. Winston fought bravely and was under fire for many hours. Much to his disappointment, however, he received no medals.

After fighting at the frontier, he returned to his regular post in southern India. Once back with his regiment, Winston hit upon a novel method of compensating for the lack of action there. He would write a book about his experiences in the northern war, which he would call *The Story of the Malakand Field Force.*

> *In years [Churchill] is a boy; in temperament he is also a boy; but in intention, in deliberate plan, purpose, adaptation of means to ends he is already a man. . . . At the rate he goes there will hardly be room for him in Parliament at thirty or in England at forty. It is a pace that cannot last, yet already he holds a vast lead of his contemporaries.*
> —GEORGE W. STEVENS
> British journalist, writing in the London *Daily Mail* in 1898

As always, Churchill threw himself into the task. He did not hesitate to speak out against British policy, or to express his fascination with warfare. Working furiously, he completed the manuscript in just seven weeks.

The book was much praised for its strong, honest style. Important government officials wrote to Churchill to commend him, and many people commented that his wisdom and understanding of human affairs were remarkable for someone only 23 years old.

By 1898 another war had captured Churchill's attention, this one in Africa, in the future nation of the Sudan. General Kitchener was campaigning against native Muslim warriors opposed to British colonial rule.

From his station in India, Churchill put his mother to work in London pulling strings so that he could join Kitchener's army. But some higher officials objected, believing Churchill wanted to go to the Sudan merely for his own glory. Fortunately, the prime minister, Lord Salisbury, had read Churchill's book and spoke out on his behalf. When he received permission to join Kitchener in the Sudan, Churchill began to hope that he might lead a troop of soldiers. In addition, the London *Morning Post* had given him a contract to write articles, and he intended to expand them eventually into yet another book.

In this war along the Nile River the British fought Muslim soldiers who wanted to secede from British-occupied Egypt and establish a separate homeland in the Sudan. The Muslims far outnumbered Kitchener's forces, which were moving slowly towards Omdurman, the Muslim capital.

It was here in the Sudan that Churchill experienced his most dangerous military action. At Omdurman he took part in a cavalry charge against the Muslim army. He acquitted himself with conspicuous bravery and was sure that he had killed at least three men. The British had suffered heavy losses during the campaign, however, and the war was to drag on for another year. Although General Kitchener became a hero, there was one incident

Transvaal President Paul ("Oom Paul") Kruger (1825–1904) was called an "ignorant, dirty, cunning old man" by British Colonial Secretary Joseph Chamberlain (1836–1914). However, Paul Kruger proved to be a tough and resourceful leader who put his faith in "God and the Mauser." (The Mauser was a high-performance rifle that greatly contributed to the Transvaal army's awesome firepower.)

that marred his brilliant record.

When his troops occupied Omdurman, Kitchener ordered that the tomb of the Mahdi, the Muslim leader who had killed Britain's General Gordon 13 years earlier, be destroyed and the man's bones thrown into the Nile River. Kitchener also ordered that the Mahdi's skull be delivered to him as a trophy. Winston described this act in detail in his articles. Kitchener, he charged, was guilty of excessive bloodlust and had killed Muslim soldiers who pleaded for mercy.

Churchill knew that his reports would cause an uproar, and they certainly did. When the gravedigging incident became known. Queen Victoria was furious. Many army officers wrote letters to the newspaper complaining that Churchill's criticism of senior officers amounted to insubordination. In fact, though Churchill had described many sides of Kitchener and definitely admired the general's skill and patience, the general was, nevertheless, a man without pity or compassion, a soldier who committed barbaric acts in the wake of his greatest victories. Though Churchill's articles caused an outcry, they gained him a reputation for honesty. In his determination to know the truth, he was also learning about the complex nature of great men.

When Churchill left the Sudan in September 1898, he was confident that by writing he could make enough money to run for the House of Commons. He returned to India to finish his tour of duty and left the army a few months later.

Churchill arrived in London in April 1899, ready to launch his political career. To run for Parliament, he needed to find a district that would be holding an election soon. As it happened, there was an available seat on the Conservative party ticket in the borough of Oldham, a centre of the textile industry with a large working-class population. He duly gained the approval of the Conservative party and was selected to stand as its candidate in the election, which was scheduled for July.

The odds were not in his favour. His opponents, the candidates of the Liberal party, were much better known to the local voters and traditionally better represented the interests of British workers, whereas Churchill was a newcomer not only to the district but to politics in general. Though he campaigned long and hard and made many speeches (in which he did little more than repeat campaign slogans he had learned from his father), Churchill lost the election. His tendency to insist that Conservative policies had improved the workers' living standards failed to convince the largely ill-fed and badly paid voters of the borough of Oldham.

Taking defeat in his stride, Churchill went to Blenheim to work on the last stages of *The River War,* a book based on his experiences in the Sudan. Away from the campaign trail he was free to think about other things and make new political connections. Events in South Africa had begun to interest him, and he sought out Joseph Chamberlain, a cabinet member who held the post of colonial secretary. Chamberlain, one of the most powerful men in the government, had been urging a buildup of British influence in South Africa.

In South Africa there was a delicate balance of power between the English and the Boers. Of the four colonies in South Africa, two were British and two were Boer republics. One of the Boer nations, Transvaal, had been taken by England in 1877, but the Transvaal Boers had regained their autonomy in 1884. Ten years later gold was discovered in Transvaal, and the newly rich country used its wealth to build up its army. Transvaal soon became hostile to England. Meanwhile, many non-Boers flocked to Transvaal to find their fortunes. These *uitlanders* (outsiders), as the Boers called them, were mostly British. The Boers hated them and refused to grant them civil rights. In 1898 Transvaal and the other Boer nation, the Orange Free State, allied themselves against the British.

Early in 1899 the *uitlanders* wrote to Queen Victoria, asking her to intervene on their behalf. The British and Boer governments agreed to meet, but for months the talks were deadlocked. While the British softened their position, the Boers held fast. By September Churchill was sure there would

Former war prisoner Churchill in Durban. Emerging from a train in Portuguese East Africa, the filthy and tattered escapee had gone straight to the British consulate, where he was refused admittance. "I," roared the brash young correspondent, "am Winston BLOODY Churchill! Come down here at once!" The startled consul hastily obliged.

35

be war. He went to the office of the London *Morning Post,* whose publishers agreed with his perception of the situation and offered him a lucrative contract as a war correspondent.

When the Boers requested that the British cease the military buildup in their own colonies, the British promptly refused. The Boer War began on October 12, 1899. Churchill shared Chamberlain's view of the war—he did not think the Boers stood a chance against the British army.

But when he arrived in South Africa on October 31, Churchill was surprised at the news he heard. The Boers had invaded the British colony of Natal and had surrounded most of the British troops, whose commander was General Sir George White. Obviously, the British had badly underestimated the Boers. Eager to reach the front, Churchill made his way to the British stronghold of Estcourt. In the course of his journey he met several old acquaintances from earlier days. From his conversations with them it became apparent that the Boers were well-equipped, highly motivated, and intended to fight long and hard for their cause.

Churchill soon had an opportunity to observe Boer capabilities for himself. Two companies of soldiers were being sent out on an armoured train to gather information. The captain, who had just been given orders to prepare his men for the mission, saw Churchill and invited him along. Churchill agreed, though both men thought the expedition foolish. As it turned out, 500 Boer cavalry spotted the train the following morning and waited for it on high ground overlooking the track. The British had played right into their hands.

Led by the brilliant Louis Botha, the Boers opened fire on the train. The civilian engineer panicked and accelerated to full speed. The train flew around a bend and crashed into some large rocks the enemy had placed on the rails.

The first three cars jumped the track, with the result that many of the troops inside were badly thrown around. The Boers pumped bullets into the train, wounding several men. Other soldiers escaped and ran for cover. Churchill, who was at the back of the train, initially considered attempting to use the locomotive to push the derailed cars right off the tracks. The locomotive could then be linked to the mobile cars at the rear of the train. This, however, proved impossible. He began carrying wounded men to the locomotive, while the Boers maintained their fire. Suddenly, a handful of Boers infiltrated to within yards of the track. An armed horseman came upon Churchill, who reached for his pistol only to discover that he had left it on the train. The intrepid reporter for the London *Morning Post* raised his hands into the air to surrender.

Churchill and the other survivors were taken to a prison camp in Pretoria, the capital of Transvaal. They arrived there on November 12, and were taken to a heavily guarded compound surrounded by a tall barbed-wire fence. Because he was a newspaper writer and a Churchill, he quickly became the most famous prisoner. He tried to use his status to get himself released, writing letter after letter to the Boer officials. But they remained unmoved by his pleas. Frustrated, he pondered alternative stratagems. Then, the captain of the failed mission took

The Boer army, determined and well equipped, proved more formidable than the British had expected. Perceiving that victory would require large numbers of fresh soldiers, Churchill decided to spur his nation's patriotism. "More irregular troops are wanted," he cabled his newspaper. "Are the gentlemen of England all fox-hunting?"

him aside and confided that he and another prisoner had drawn up a plan to escape. When asked if he would join them, Churchill, without hesitating, said he would.

The plan was a good one. The two men had collected money and a map of the city, and one of them spoke both the Boer tongue, Afrikaans. They decided to make their escape on December 12.

"There are three of us to go," the captain said, "and we will certainly do so if the chance is favourable." But when they checked the guard post at the latrines it became apparent that the sentry on duty was exercising extreme vigilance.

Despite the risk, Churchill could wait no longer. Taking advantage of a moment's inattention on the part of the guard, Churchill leapt from the window of the outhouse. Disguised in his civilian suit, he strolled past several other guards and began his great and arduous journey to Portuguese East Africa. From there he made his way by ship to Durban, the main port of the British southern African colony of Natal. Greeted as a hero, he made one of his best speeches from the steps of city hall. His name was in all the headlines, and his bravery was widely hailed.

Eager to get back into action and in a uniform this time, Churchill then departed for the British post near Estcourt, whence the armoured train had set out on its ill-fated mission a few weeks earlier. Though Churchill was still technically employed by the newspaper, the general commanding British forces in Natal, Sir Redvers Buller, agreed to give him an unpaid commission.

The British had to contend with a string of defeats at the hands of the Boers, who used not only irregular methods like guerrilla warfare but also made expert use of up-to-date military technology. They massacred the British with equipment that Churchill's countrymen considered newfangled and "unsporting." The Boers had purchased machine guns and long-range artillery from several European countries. In one of the war's worst crises, 16,000 men under General Sir George White were besieged by Boer forces at Ladysmith in western Natal.

> *The most durable structures raised in stone by the strength of man, the mightiest monuments of his power, crumble into dust, while the words spoken with fleeting breath, the passing expression of the unstable fancies of his mind, endure not as echoes of the past, not as mere archaeological curiosities or venerable relics, but with a force and life as new and strong, and sometimes far stronger than when they were first spoken, and leaping across the gulf of three thousand years, they light the world for us today.*
> —WINSTON CHURCHILL
> addressing authors, 1908

Hundreds were dying of dysentery and starvation because no relief force could break through the Boer lines.

Finally, by the end of February 1900, the British position improved. Their sheer weight of numbers began to tell upon the Boers, who gradually fell back. Ladysmith was relieved on February 28, 1900, and Churchill rode with the first formations to enter the city.

Churchill had undoubtedly made his mark in South Africa. An agent offered to arrange a lecture tour of America for him and many magazines wanted to employ him as a writer. In addition, he was planning to write a book about his experiences in the Boer War.

In June the British finally took Pretoria, the capital of Transvaal. Churchill took part in one last battle a week later and then decided that it was time to leave South Africa.

In this short, exciting period of his life, Churchill had done exactly what he had set out to do—he had earned the fame that would serve as the foundation for a career in politics. And his writing would serve to finance that career.

By openly chasing medals and seeking glory, Churchill had managed to alienate many of his colleagues and superiors in the military. Despite this, by fighting in three wars and putting himself to the test each time, he had gained a reputation for bravery. Indeed, there were those who respected him for his wisdom and ambition, and looked on him as a young, if somewhat eccentric and unorthodox, genius. Churchill had done more in only 25 years than many people manage in a lifetime—and yet he remained impatient for greater success, for achievements of a different, higher order.

> *All my dreams of comradeship with him, of entering Parliament at his side and in his support, were ended. There remained for me only to pursue his aims and vindicate his memory.*
> —WINSTON CHURCHILL writing about the death of his father, Randolph Churchill, in his book *My Early Life*

DARE
TO BE
FREE
THE VOTE
THE VOTE
THE VOTE
THE VOTE
VOTES FOR WOMEN

3
In His Father's Footsteps

> *Real leaders of men do not come forward offering to lead. They show the way, and when it has been found to lead to victory they accept as a matter of course the allegiance of those who have followed.*
> —WINSTON CHURCHILL

Churchill returned to London late in the summer of 1900. Eager to run for Parliament now that he was out of the army, he returned to Oldham to campaign for election, even though he had lost there a year earlier. The main issue of political debate at that time was the Boer War, which Churchill, as the Conservative party candidate, fully supported. In the eyes of the voters, Churchill really did stand for the war—his famous escape was just what he needed to become a Member of Parliament! On October 1, 1900, Conservative party candidate Winston Churchill became the Member of Parliament for Oldham. For Churchill, the fact that he had won by a mere 22 votes in no way diminished the joy he felt at having fulfiled his dream at last. He had gained his first political victory and would "sit" in the House of Commons when the next session convened in February.

In the meantime, Churchill embarked on a lecture tour of Britain and the United States. His American agent introduced him as "the hero of five wars, the author of six books, and the future prime minister of Britain." While the British engagements

Colonial Secretary Joseph Chamberlain enraged Churchill with his anti-free trade views, setting off a year of debate between the former allies. ("Mr. Chamberlain," said Churchill, "loves the working man. He loves to see him work.") Chamberlain was permanently crippled by a stroke after his resounding defeat in the 1903 election.

Suffragettes (activists for women's right to vote) campaign in 1900. Before 1912, when he backed a bill that sought to secure the vote for women, Churchill was vehemently attacked by the suffragette movement, which he had called "contrary to natural law." British women over 21 were granted full voting rights in 1928.

41

Clementine Hozier (1885–1977) and Winston Churchill a week before their 1908 wedding. "Clemmie" was known for her classic beauty, her hunting skill, her pronounced likes and firm dislikes (one of which was Winston's mother), her strong suffragette views, and her adoration of the brilliant but unpredictable man she married.

> *[He] can best be described as one of those orators who, before they get up, do not know what they are going to say; when they are speaking, do not know what they are saying; and when they have sat down, do not know what they have said.*
> —WINSTON CHURCHILL
> criticizing a political opponent

were a great success, his appearances in America proved less profitable since the agent charged an extremely high commission. Nevertheless, Churchill managed to make the money he needed to begin his career without financial worry. When Parliament opened its doors on February 14, 1901, Churchill proudly entered the halls that would be his home for more than half a century.

There were in Parliament many ancient rules of procedure that tended to confuse new members. But Churchill had done his homework, learning all the fine points of the right way to speak and the protocol that had to be observed. From the start he was outspoken and ambitious. When he made his maiden speech, the chamber was filled to overflowing.

As a Conservative, Churchill naturally intended to keep faith with the party that had elected him. Yet he knew that the Conservatives lacked unity and saw very clearly that he would gain little distinction by simply following the party line. His outspoken criticism of government policy in South Africa ruffled the feathers of many of his parliamentary colleagues. Joseph Chamberlain, the powerful Conservative colonial secretary who had befriended him, became visibly annoyed as the young politician warmed to his task.

But Churchill, exhibiting his characteristic independence of mind, was determined to speak the truth as he saw it. He sincerely believed that the Conservatives were making one mistake after another. As things turned out, Churchill's first speech in Parliament hinted at the disillusionment with Conservative policies that would increasingly trouble him during the next three years. His initial ties to the Conservative party had much to do with the fact that his father had belonged to it. As he gained greater experience and maturity, these emotional ties grew weaker. By the end of 1903 Churchill had to face the fact that his personal convictions had more in common with the philosophy of the Liberal party. As a Liberal, Churchill thought, he could accomplish more, and follow policies he believed in. He also suspected that Liberal affiliations would enable him to achieve prominence much faster.

The Conservatives, he felt, had not taken a sufficiently strong stand on the issues that he thought especially important. Their proposals to abandon free trade and impose a tax on imports shocked Churchill, who was certain that it would hurt British prosperity. In May 1904 Churchill left the Conservative party, and took his place on the Liberal benches. The switch, although not without risk, came as a great relief to him. When the Conservative government fell at the end of 1905 and a new one headed by Liberals was formed, Churchill gained his first senior appointment. At only 31, he was made undersecretary of state for the colonies, a position that would greatly aid him in any future bid to become a full-fledged cabinet minister.

During his two-year stay at the Colonial Office, Churchill was second-in-command to Lord Elgin over matters concerning Britain's overseas possessions. At the time, the colonies were the major focus of attention in Parliament. As usual, Churchill took great care to keep himself in the spotlight.

He made it his business to know everything that was going on. He soon became known for his ambition and for his boundless energy. Though Churchill sometimes made it difficult for Lord Elgin by constantly drawing attention to himself, he admired the older man. They worked well together, and, among other outstanding achievements, laid the foundation for the unification of South Africa, which

Hurrying across London in 1910, David Lloyd George (1863–1945) is flanked by his wife and Churchill (third from left). Churchill's feelings about the fiery Welsh politician were ambivalent, but his respect outweighed his misgivings. He used the words "master and servant" to refer to Lloyd George and himself. "I," he said, "was the servant."

> *To say that Protection means a greater development of wealth is an economic delusion, and to say that Protection means a fairer distribution of wealth is unspeakable humbug.*
> —WINSTON CHURCHILL
> arguing in favor of
> free trade in 1903

London policemen await reinforcements during a battle with eastern European revolutionaries in January 1911. Attacked in Parliament for having visited the scene of the fighting, Churchill admitted that, as home secretary, he should not have done so. But, he said, he had found it impossible to stay away when events were so uncertain "and, moreover, were extremely interesting."

had been so scarred by the Boer War. After helping draft a new constitution for Transvaal, Churchill made a strong, statesmanlike appeal to the Conservatives in Parliament. He persuaded them that granting self-governing status to Transvaal did not mean that British troops had died for nothing in the Boer War. This piece of diplomacy was the crowning achievement of Churchill's collabouration with Lord Elgin.

Early in 1908 a new Liberal prime minister took office who would govern Britain during one of the most turbulent periods in its history. For his good work at the Colonial Office, Herbert Asquith rewarded Churchill with a promotion to cabinet rank. He was to preside over the Board of Trade. Churchill accepted the offer with pride. At 33, he was three years younger than his father had been when given his first cabinet appointment.

At about the same time as he took office at the Board of Trade, Churchill found himself in another new situation: He was in love. At a dinner party in early March, he happened to sit next to a beautiful 23-year-old woman named Clementine Hozier. Men flocked after Clemmie, as she was called, but Churchill was determined to win her. Now that he had money, a cabinet post, and a promising future, he was in a position to consider marriage. Churchill courted Clemmie with his famous determination, sending her an endless succession of admiring letters. Finally, on an August weekend at Blenheim, his grandparents' estate, he proposed and she accepted.

Winston Churchill and Clementine Hozier were married in London on September 12, 1908. Clemmie was a lovely and nervous bride, but she was not as nervous as Winston, who looked pale and was talking politics up to the moment the ceremony began.

In later years, Churchill often spoke of his marriage as his greatest achievement. He and Clemmie were to know much happiness together for 57 years. Clemmie was a supportive partner to Winston, and she took an active interest in all his affairs. Together they raised four children, three girls and a boy.

It was not an easy move from the Colonial Office to the Board of Trade, but Churchill made it gracefully. In his new post he was now in charge of labour negotiations and trade matters.

It was during this period that Churchill made an alliance that was one of the most important of his career. His new mentor was David Lloyd George, then Chancellor of the Exchequer. Lloyd George was a Liberal too, and Churchill idolized him.

Churchill and Lloyd George became a team and between them put through much progressive legislation. Churchill established state-run labour exchanges, offices that kept track of employment opportunities and made such information available to the jobless. Together they also launched a major attack on the vastly inflated defence budget, arguing that military estimates should be reduced and the resultant savings spent on social programmes. This caused an uproar in the government, especially when they asked for a reduction in spending for the navy. England had been a major sea power for hundreds of years, and now Churchill and Lloyd George proposed limiting battleship construction to four vessels rather than the six requested by Britain's admirals. Others in the government, including Prime Minister Asquith, strenuously opposed their recommendations. Many politicians felt that Britain's military capability should be kept at least as strong as that of Germany, where a substantial arms buildup was under way.

In their unceasing search for new sources of revenue Churchill and Lloyd George came up with a particularly controversial measure in April 1909. They suggested taxing the rich and using that money to fund social programmemes. Since such legislation would basically mean a redistribution of wealth, Churchill immediately came under attack from the members of his own class, the British aristocracy. This issue of reform caused a major uproar, for it meant great changes in Britain's traditional social order. The members of the House of Lords registered their sense of outrage with particular vehemence since it was their property that would be taxed most heavily should the budget pass.

The Socialism of the Christian era. . . was based on the idea that 'all mine is yours,' but the Socialism of Mr. Grayson [a socialist M.P.] is based on the idea that 'all yours is mine.'
—WINSTON CHURCHILL
speaking in 1908

Striking Welsh coal miners in 1910. Home Secretary Churchill ordered the policemen he sent to the scene not to fire, but union leaders blamed him for the deaths of two miners anyway. In later years, he was often jeered by working men who wrongly believed he had ordered a massacre in Wales.

The Sidney Street, London, hideout of the armed eastern European radicals who were cornered by the British police in January 1911 blazed for an hour before Home Secretary Churchill allowed the fire engines near it. There were no survivors. "I thought it better to let the house burn down," he said later, "than spend good British lives in rescuing those ferocious rascals."

The dispute over the budget caused a split in the government, and new elections were held. Despite a major reduction in the Liberals' majority, Asquith and his party came out on top yet again.

Because of his increasing political ability and maturity, Churchill was appointed to preside over the Home Office, which was responsible for such matters as the prison system, the police, social welfare, and internal security.

Just as Churchill went to serve at the Home Office, Britain crowned a new king. In the spring of 1910, King Edward VII died at age 68 and his son came to the throne as George V. It was the end of an era. Edward had stood for the conservative traditions of the aristocrats and wealthy businessmen who had dominated the country for centuries.

At the Home Office, where he stayed for only 20 months, Churchill made his mark and exercised greater power than he had in any of his previous positions. Setting out to reform the prison system, he began by abolishing corporal (physical) punishment, instituting repayment schedules in place of imprisonment for nonpayment of fines, and introducing educational programs for convicts. He also took it upon himself personally to review many individual cases of prison injustice.

Churchill faced several crises while at the Home Office. Welsh miners went on strike over wages, and the local police requested assistance from the military when the strikers began to make their point by damaging private property. Churchill sent in 300 London policemen and 400 troops, and order was soon restored.

Churchill was criticized for his actions by both rightists and leftists—the former said he had done too little, the latter claimed that he had done too much. But there were more tests to come. In January 1911 Churchill received an urgent telephone call. A gang of eastern European revolutionaries had been surrounded in a building on Sidney Street, in London's East End, an area which housed the majority of the city's immigrant population. These refugees from satellite states of the autocratic Russian Empire had already killed three London policemen and had staged many robberies to finance their revolutionary struggle. Churchill sent in troops to reinforce the police and then went to survey the situation for himself. When the building went up in flames Churchill refused to allow the fire services to deal with the blaze. His presence at the scene was severely criticized by the press and by his colleagues in Parliament. The Liberals became the target of violent public protest since their refusal to tighten up immigration laws had allowed vast numbers of politically suspect foreigners to settle in the country.

In the summer of 1911 the Asquith government found itself confronted with yet another crisis. Labour unrest had spread throughout Britain and culminated in August with a strike by railway workers. Churchill took action immediately, realizing that without a rail service the country would be crippled. To keep the trains running, he sent 50,000 soldiers to stations around the country. While many people disliked Churchill's willingness to break strikes by deploying the military, few chose to notice that almost no violence occurred during his interventions.

In late 1911 the focus of attention had begun to shift to foreign affairs. It was clear that Germany was beginning to take a hostile position towards France. Popular debate centred on Britain's options in the event of a European war. Lloyd George sincerely felt that Britain should oppose Germany. Though few people thought there would actually be a war, the atmosphere had definitely changed.

Churchill wanted the prestigious position of First Lord of the Admiralty. In that capacity he would be

Sir John Fisher (1841–1920), who was First Sea Lord from 1904 to 1910, had been furious when, in 1908, Home Secretary Churchill, calling the idea of war with Germany "nonsense," had opposed Fisher's request for six more battleships and had declared that four would suffice. In 1911, however, as First Lord of the Admiralty, Churchill agreed with Fisher. Together, the former opponents made the Royal Navy a formidable fighting force.

On Britain's Royal Navy, wrote Churchill, "floated the might, majesty, dominion, and power of the British Empire." In 1911, as the nation's new civilian navy chief, he said his number-one priority was to put the fleet into "a state of instant . . . readiness for war."

> *While large numbers of persons enjoy great wealth, while the mass of the artisan classes are abreast of and in advance of their fellows in other lands, there is a minority, considerable in numbers, whose condition is a disgrace to a scientific and professedly Christian civilization, and constitutes a grave and increasing peril to the state.*
> —WINSTON CHURCHILL discussing unemployment, 1908

German troops invade Belgium in 1914. Churchill had spoken for his countrymen when he said of the Sarajevo assassination, "Balkan quarrels are no vital concern of ours." The incident, however, triggered a chain of events that pushed Britain toward the bloodiest conflict the world had ever known.

responsible for defining and directing Britain's naval policy. In September 1911 Prime Minister Asquith agreed to have him transferred from the Home Office to the Admiralty. Nothing could have made Churchill happier.

Even though Churchill had fought to cut military expenditure in the past, making the navy ready for war was now his first priority. It was a big job, and not an easy one; only time would tell how successful he would be.

As soon as he assumed his duties at the Admiralty, Churchill began to study maps, inspect ships, and learn all he could. In his determination to create the best possible British navy, Churchill made some unpopular decisions. He replaced many admirals that he considered incompetent, and pressed for increases in the naval budget at a time when many cabinet ministers were reluctant to approve such measures.

Britain's fleet was the country's first line of defence, and was constantly in need of modernizing. After intensive discussions with Admiral Sir John Fisher, a naval officer of great ability and experience, Churchill decided to pursue his recommendations. He ordered that Britain's fleet convert from coal to oil power and that the ships be fitted with much heavier guns. Britain also needed many more battleships so as to keep up with the rapidly expanding German navy.

Tensions increased immensely over the next two and a half years. The German fleet was obviously preparing for war, and Churchill continued to fight for increases in the naval budget. He even lost the support of Lloyd George, who remained unconvinced that Germany intended to go to war. By late 1913, when Churchill requested the greatest naval expenditures in British history, nearly everyone seemed to be against him. He came under increasing pressure to resign.

In June 1914 festivities took place in Germany marking the opening of a new canal that would give German warships faster access to the North Sea. The celebrations were interrupted, however, by some alarming news. The heir to the throne of

Austria-Hungary, Archduke Franz Ferdinand, had been assassinated by a Serb in the city of Sarajevo.

This was the first in a chain of events that led to World War I. Austria, an ally of Germany, gave Serbia an ultimatum. It was so provocative that many European politicians considered Austria likely to invade. Since Austria was formally allied with Germany, and Serbia had a similar understanding with Russia, there was every prospect of a war between the two greatest powers in central Europe. France was bound by treaty to aid Russia in the event of conflict and Britain had unofficially agreed to aid France. Germany declared war on France on August 3. On July 31 the German Chancellor, von Bethmann-Hollweg, had announced that his nation's armed forces would not respect Belgian neutrality in the march on France. British involvement became absolutely inevitable since Great Britain was pledged to the defence of Belgium. The army and navy were mobilized.

Churchill, horrified at the idea of war in Europe, was excited nonetheless. During his three years as First Lord of the Admiralty, he had prepared his nation's navy for the possibility of war.

Finally, on August 4, 1914, Germany invaded Belgium on the pretext that France was planning to attack Germany. This, however, was untrue. When Prime Minister Asquith received the news, he knew it was Britain's turn to issue an ultimatum. If the Germans failed to announce an intention to withdraw from Belgium, England would consider itself at war with Germany at 11:00 P.M. London time on August 4, 1914.

The hours passed, and no reply came. When the ultimatum expired, Churchill had the message "Commence hostilities with Germany" telegraphed to every British warship and naval base. A few minutes later he left Admiralty House for No. 10, Downing Street, the official London residence of British prime ministers. There he took his place alongside his cabinet colleagues in accordance with a custom that required ministers of state to report to the prime minister immediately following the outbreak of war.

Austria's Archduke Franz Ferdinand (1863–1914) and his wife Sophie (1868–1914), greet a government official in the Bosnian town of Sarajevo on June 28, 1914. Moments later, they were both shot dead by a Serbian nationalist, and Europe, as Churchill said in a letter to his wife, was "trembling on the verge of a general war."

> *At thirty-four [Churchill] stands before the country as the most interesting figure in politics, his life a crowded drama of action, his courage high, his vision unclouded, his boats burned.*
> —A. G. GARDINER
> British journalist, writing in 1908

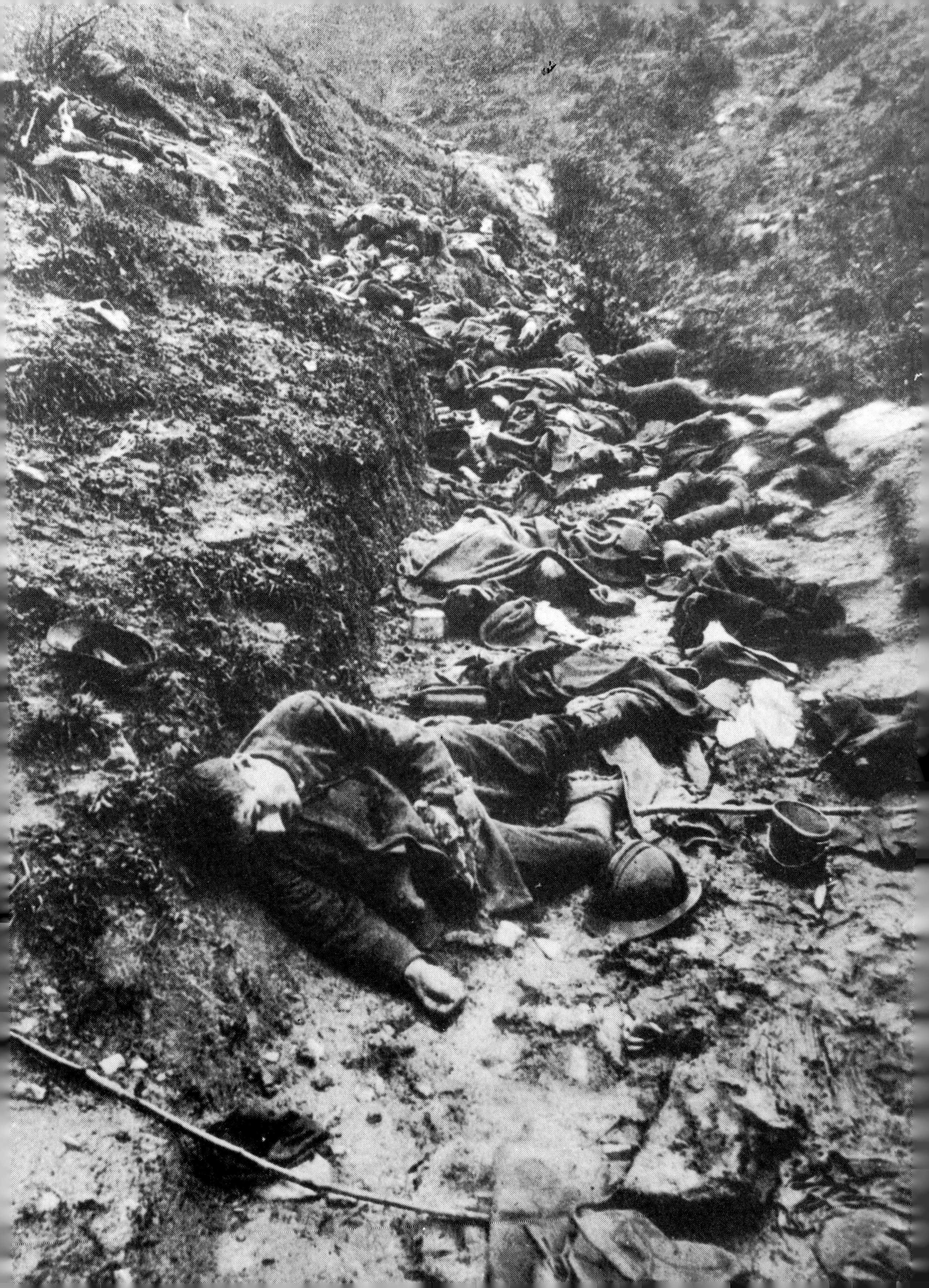

4
The War to End All Wars

> *Before the war it had seemed incredible that such terrors and slaughters, even if they began, could last more than a few months. After the first two years it was difficult to believe that they would ever end. We seemed separated from the old life by a measureless gulf.*
> —WINSTON CHURCHILL
> in his *The World Crisis,*
> *1916–1918*

Britain was at war in Europe for the first time in 100 years. The British army was ready for action and the navy Churchill had prepared was vigorously patrolling millions of square miles of the world's oceans.

The blood was racing in Churchill's veins. His love for the "noble cause" of war had not diminished since the days when he had commanded nothing but troops of toy soldiers. Eager to play a leading part in the devising of grand strategy, he made his views known at War Council meetings. He stressed that Britain had to show the Germans just who was master of the seas. He believed that an early major triumph would shorten the war.

The War Council consisted of Prime Minister Asquith, his cabinet, and his military advisers. General Kitchener, under whom Churchill had served in the Sudan, was now secretary of state for war. Though he and Churchill respected each other, they often clashed over questions of policy.

The great victory at sea that Churchill so desperately desired did not come immediately. World War I was destined to be fought mainly on land. Even at the outset, Kitchener sensed that it would be a

British soldiers lie dead and dying in one of the thousands of muddy trenches that crisscrossed the fields of France and Flanders during World War I. Trench fighting, with its mines and poison gas, baffled the British high command, whose officers had been trained in a period when chivalry, not technology, had dominated military thinking.

The stern face and pointing finger of Lord Kitchener appeared on recruiting posters all over Britain after he became secretary of state for war in 1914. Although he and Churchill had frequently disagreed in the past, Churchill said he found Kitchener "much more affable" than he had expected.

51

> *Now, God be thanked Who has matched us with His hour, / And caught our youth, and wakened us from sleeping.*
> —RUPERT BROOKE
> British poet, celebrating the renewed sense of purpose that he and others of his generation felt upon the outbreak of World War I

Workers in a British munitions factory in 1916. British forces were handicapped by ammunition shortages in the first year of the war, but when Lloyd George took over the Ministry of Munitions in 1915, he built 95 factories. He was hailed as "the one man who can win the war."

long war. He proposed that a British Expeditionary Force of six divisions (80,000 men) be sent to France as quickly and secretly as possible. Transporting these men and their horses and supplies across the English Channel turned out to be the British navy's greatest achievement in the early stages of the war. In an operation that took just 10 days the entire force was ferried to France with no adverse incidents or casualties.

War fever swept through Britain and thousands of young men lined up to volunteer for service. Most young Britons at that time were willing to fight in their country's wars, and die if necessary. Few people had foreseen that the technological advances in weaponry over the previous 50 years would change the face of war forever. World War I would prove to be the first "modern" war. The age of mass slaughter had arrived.

From the outset, the war had been fought in the trenches of a front that stretched across northeastern France. As the casualty lists grew longer and the fighting remained both bloody and inconclusive, Churchill worried that Kitchener had perhaps been right—this might well be a long and murderous war. During those early weeks Churchill regularly visited the front to advise the generals about strategy decided in the War Council or to give them his expert opinion on how things ought to be done. Churchill's almost boyish enthusiasm and determination only served to convince his cabinet colleagues that such visits did not so much serve the war effort as interfere with it. They suggested that Churchill restrict himself to Admiralty business. But Churchill was never content to do one job at a time. And besides, of all the cabinet ministers, he alone saw the war as it was—a dirty and ruthless conflict, quite unlike any that Britain had ever faced before.

It was a war in which Churchill, always eager to engage the enemy, would argue for the bold strategy, only to end up making many costly errors. In a hasty move, he and Kitchener decided to send British reinforcements to Antwerp, the most strongly fortified port in Belgium. The city was already reeling beneath a savage German bombardment and the inadequately trained naval infantry brigades that Churchill sent in were quickly brushed aside by their more seasoned opponents. Churchill was harshly criticized for this defeat. Worse yet, despite the supposed invincibility of the recently modernized navy, the British were losing at sea. Several new vessels had been sunk by German submarines.

By the end of 1914 things were going badly for the British and for Churchill. By constantly interfering with the conduct of operations in France he had angered Kitchener. Additionally, the many British losses at sea were being blamed on poor planning by Churchill's office. There had been no really major naval success except for the safe transportation of the British Expeditionary Force.

It had become increasingly obvious that the war in Europe was utterly bogged down in the trenches of France. Churchill began to press for a diversionary attack on a German ally in a different theatre of operations. He was not alone in suggesting such a move—everyone in the cabinet had a different spot they thought would be best.

In this desperate atmosphere Winston Churchill helped launch the mission that turned out to be one of Britain's greatest wartime disasters. At the eastern end of the Mediterranean Sea was Turkey, which had signed an alliance with Germany. Ironically, this unlikely alliance was Churchill's fault. In July 1914 he had impounded two recently completed Turkish battleships in the British shipyards where they had been built. The Turkish government, outraged, immediately signed a secret agreement with Germany. It is entirely possible that had Churchill not acted in such a high-handed manner, Turkey might have entered the war on Britain's side. Indeed, the Turks had sought an alliance with the British Empire in 1911 but Churchill had told them that they had ideas "above their station." Turkey bordered on Russia, which was an ally of England and France. By late 1914 Grand Duke Nicholas of Russia had warned the British that he might be forced to withdraw troops from the eastern European front to face the Turkish

> *What is our task? To make Britain a country fit for heroes to live in. . . . There is no time to lose.*
> —DAVID LLOYD GEORGE
> speaking in 1918

Beaming with confidence, Britons line up to enlist in 1915. Patriotism in Britain was at its height during World War I, stirred by poems and popular music-hall songs like "Oh, We Don't Want to Lose You, But We Think You Ought to Go."

Visibly fatigued, French soldiers stand at the entrance to their dugout during a lull in the fighting. Because both sides were firmly dug into their trench networks, the conflict remained largely inconclusive until shortly before the end of the war. The casualties, however, were appalling: by 1918, when the war ended, more than 10 million soldiers had been killed.

threat to southern Russia. The British realized that a Russian change of tactics would release thousands of German troops for action against the already hard-pressed Allied forces in France. The need for British action in the eastern Mediterranean now seemed paramount.

Kitchener debated the issue with Churchill. Was there any way, he asked, that the British navy could support a land action that would decisively disrupt the Turkish war effort? Churchill said that the only possible stratagem was to force a passage through the Dardanelles, a narrow strait on the tip of the Turkish mainland and the gateway to the ancient capital city of Constantinople (now Istanbul) and the Black Sea. But it was a dangerous idea, and even Churchill was uncertain as to the feasibility of such a project.

The Dardanelles were heavily mined and the Turks had a formidable system of gun batteries and forts commanding the strait. Churchill asked the opinion of Vice-Admiral Sackville Carden, the commander of the squadron that was blockading the exits from the Dardanelles so as to prevent German and Turkish naval units from breaking out into the Mediterranean Sea.

Carden replied that forcing a passage through the strait would require an extended operation undertaken by many ships. Since few people back in London had been convinced that such a mission could succeed, the fact that the admiral had not dismissed the question out of hand gave Churchill and his faction reasonable grounds for hope. In a second communication Carden said that the entire operation would take about a month and he outlined his proposed plan of attack.

Churchill became excited about the possibility of pulling off the manoeuvre. Concluding that the risk of casualties would be low, the War Council approved the operation, hoping that it would mark the turning point of the war. Asquith set aside his personal reservations and signed an order authorizing the expedition. So elated were the majority of Britain's planners at the prospect of changing the course of the war with a single bold stroke that no one looked too hard at the many obvious risks of the mission.

An Allied naval squadron was readied to force the Dardanelles, bombard the Gallipoli peninsula, and then move on to take Constantinople. Soon, however, the first note of caution was sounded. Kitchener believed that ground forces would be needed in order to consolidate the gains made by the initial naval bombardment. Even as the War Council debated the issue of sending troops, alerted the available formations, and argued among themselves, the task force commenced its daring and desperate action. In the teeth of a winter gale, eight British and four French battleships ploughed through heavy seas to the mouth of the strait and began shelling the Turkish forts just before 10:00 A.M. on February 19, 1915.

At first, it appeared that the mission might succeed. The navy destroyed several forts at the west-

A World War I German submarine. These vessels, known as U-boats (an abbreviation of *Unterseeboot*, German for undersea boat), sank dozens of British warships and freighters. The U-boats' torpedoing of American commercial shipping in 1917 brought the United States into the war that same year.

ern end of the strait. But as soon as the British fleet started to move through the strait, the Turkish and German gunners began pounding at the battleships. The fleet pulled back.

Churchill was still pushing for a decisive effort, and on March 18 the combined fleet moved into the strait under the command of Vice-Admiral John de Robeck. Admiral Carden had almost collapsed under the strain just two days earlier and had resigned his command on the advice of his doctor. De Robeck believed that if all went well they could force the strait that day and move right in to Constantinople. However, several battleships were put out of action by mines.

Dismayed by this unexpected reversal, the admirals held back from launching a second assault. They were unaware that by this time the Dardanelles batteries had run out of ammunition and the Turkish government was on the verge of abandoning Constantinople. When British land forces finally entered the battle, however, the Turks were ready. They had used the five-week interval between de Robeck's assault and the first British landings to consolidate their defences throughout the Gallipoli peninsula. Massive shipments of heavy

HMS *Cornwallis* exchanges fire with the Turks in the Dardanelles on March 18, 1915. The British fleet was the biggest ever assembled in these waters, but its mission was a failure. The Turks lost four of their 176 heavy guns; the British lost three battleships and 700 men.

British wounded are transported from Gallipoli. Poet Rupert Brooke (1887–1915) spoke for many of his countrymen in "The Soldier," written before he embarked for Gallipoli: "If I should die, think only this of me: / That there's some corner of a foreign field / That is forever England."

weapons had arrived from Germany via neutral Romania.

British losses were heavy from the start—many men failed to make it as far as the shore. When, after much bloody fighting, the British finally established beachheads, their hopes of an easy victory quickly evaporated. Though the British had anticipated otherwise, the Turks proved themselves determined warriors. The Dardanelles campaign became as bogged down in trenches as had the war in France. The battle lasted six months and the British gained nothing. The operation, which ultimately cost 214,000 killed and wounded, was finally discontinued in December 1915. The Dardanelles mission had been an utter disaster. Rather than drain German military reserves, it had severely sapped British fighting strength and dealt a considerable blow to national morale.

Even though the entire War Council had approved the mission, Churchill suffered much of the blame for the Dardanelles tragedy. A public outcry accused

> *I have always urged fighting wars and other contentions with might and main till overwhelming victory, and then offering the hand of friendship to the vanquished. Thus I have always been against the Pacifists during the quarrel, and against the Jingoes at its close.*
> —WINSTON CHURCHILL

> *Russia is being rapidly reduced by the Bolsheviks to an animal form of barbarism. . . . The Bolsheviks maintain themselves by bloody and wholesale butcheries and murders. . . . Civilization is being completely extinguished over gigantic areas, while Bolsheviks hop and caper like troops of ferocious baboons amid the ruins of cities and the corpses of their victims.*
> —WINSTON CHURCHILL
> speaking at Dundee in 1918

him of poor judgment. Prime Minister Asquith, whose entire administration was losing credibility with the electorate, relieved Churchill of his job at the Admiralty and gave him the minor post of chancellor of the duchy of Lancaster.

Churchill became very depressed in the wake of this fall from grace. He was haunted by the vision of the victory that might have been achieved at the Dardanelles and saddened by the grim reality. Though he was still a member of the War Council and had a seat in Parliament, his opinions no longer counted for very much. He felt friendless and betrayed.

After a few listless months, Churchill resigned as chancellor of the duchy of Lancaster on November 11, 1915. Determined to be of some practical use, he decided to follow his instincts and return to the army. He would fight in France and face whatever fate awaited him.

The senior commanders at the front viewed Churchill as little more than a nuisance and did not give him an enthusiastic welcome. His application to lead a brigade was rejected, and he had to be content with following orders as a lieutenant colo-

Churchill (wearing a borrowed French helmet) in France in 1915. He had arrived at the front with cigars, brandy, and comfortable camping equipment. His commanding officer, who was not impressed, said, "I am afraid we have had to cut down your kit, rather," and allowed Churchill to keep no more than a spare pair of socks and his shaving gear about him while on duty.

A British Mark V tank undergoes testing at a proving ground in southern England during World War I. Churchill, always enthusiastic about new weapons, ordered the construction of Britain's first tanks in 1915. To confuse German spies, the devices were said to be water containers for the Russian army; thus they acquired the name "tanks."

nel. Churchill thus gained firsthand experience of the horrors of life in the trenches. Before long, however, he was eager to get back to the battlefield that suited him best—Parliament.

In May 1916 Churchill returned home to London and his seat in the House of Commons. Shortly after his return, Asquith resigned and Lloyd George became prime minister.

In 1917 Lloyd George appointed Churchill to a post where he could put into practice his numerous ideas for upgrading Britain's armaments. As minister of munitions he was determined to increase the production of "masses of guns, mountains of shells, clouds of aeroplanes." He also encouraged and supervised the development of the tank. Unfortunately, this revolutionary addition to military technology was received with scant enthusiasm by Britain's generals. They distrusted new inventions and continued to ignore them even when it was apparent that such machines could prove decisive. The success of a British tank attack at Cambrai in 1917, which netted 10,000 German prisoners at a cost of 1,500 British casualties, was repeated just once, in August 1918. Had the British military establishment understood the potential of the tank as profoundly as did Churchill, it is possible that a decision could have been forced in France much sooner.

The "war to end all wars" finally ground to an exhausted halt in 1918. The fight had at last gone in the Allies' favour following the arrival of over a million fresh American troops. The Germans were defeated, but for Britain and France, which had suffered 6.8 million casualties between them, it was a joyless victory. Churchill, who was named secretary of state for war and air in January 1919, gradually regained some of his former prominence. He let it be known that, although he thought the defeated Germans should pay reparations, the scale of reparations should not be so excessive as to inflame the German nation against the Allied powers. He also spoke out against Britain's former ally, Russia, where a communist revolution had overthrown the monarchy.

Allied intervention in the civil war raging between Russia's communists and monarchists had begun in 1918. The Allies favoured the monarchists out of both political conviction and resentment of the fact that Russia's new communist rulers had signed a separate peace with Germany. Churchill repeatedly called upon the government to expand the British presence in Russia. By 1921 his anti-communist barrage was little more than a one-

Communist militiamen patrol the streets of Petrograd following the Russian Revolution of 1917. Churchill could not resign himself to the fact that communists had come to power in Russia. "Civilization," he insisted, "is being extinguished ... while Bolsheviks (the most radical Russian communists) hop and caper like troops of ferocious baboons amid the ruins of cities and the corpses of their victims."

British soldiers round up Irish revolutionaries in 1920. Churchill's attitude toward the Irish gradually changed from antipathy ("What a diabolical streak they have in their character!") to respect. In 1921 he complimented Irish leaders on their "spirit and personal courage . . . in confronting the enemies of free speech and fair play."

man crusade and only ended when Lloyd George decided that Soviet Russia had become a fact of political life. He proceeded to sign a trade agreement with the regime that Winston considered "a nest of vipers" and a "vile group of cosmopolitan fanatics."

In 1921 Churchill was appointed to head the Colonial Office. In this capacity he helped bring a measure of peace to Ireland, where factions loyal to Britain had been fighting it out with Irish republicans for several years. Many Britons had been killed in Ireland while fighting the republicans and had earned the undying hatred of many Irishmen for the severity of their policing. Winston helped draft a constitution for what then became the Irish Free State, a British dominion ruled by a governor who represented the monarch. His official involvement in the turbulent politics of Ireland placed him at personal risk during the period, since at one point his name was discovered at the top of an Irish Republican Army assassination list. As secretary of state for the colonies Churchill also played a part in settling Arab affairs in the British territories of the Middle East. Though he was again in a position of some power, he still yearned for more.

> *Socialism is one of the oldest and most often expounded delusions and fallacies which this world has ever been afflicted by. It consists not merely in a general levelling of mankind, but in keeping them level once they have been beaten down.*
> —WINSTON CHURCHILL
> speaking in 1922

SHAVING
UNEMPLOYED EX SERVICE ME
Demand WORK
Not "DOLES"
HOXTON & ST LUKES
BRANCH
WE'VE DONE OUR
BIT FOR YOU.
DO JUSTICE TO US.

5
The Uneasy Peace

> *Though [Churchill] never was disinclined to take office, a refusal to compromise in order to get it kept him out of it for eleven years; and if it be objected that he has often changed his party, I would be prepared to argue that the changes have been only to suit unchanging views.*
> —COLIN COOTE
> British journalist

In 1922, amid growing unrest in Britain, Lloyd George's Liberal government fell from power. It had paid the price for failing to adapt to new divisions in British society. It had become a party without a position at a time of increasing class conflict. The Conservatives won 345 seats in Parliament, Lloyd George's "National" Liberals 62, Asquith's regular Liberals 54, and the rapidly growing Labour party 142. The Labourites, who represented the interests of the working class, now became the principal opposition party. Thus, the Liberal political tradition became outdated, socialism had found a voice in Parliament, and the British political landscape had changed forever. Churchill, already disillusioned with the Liberal party, reacted to this new configuration by becoming more conservative. As a result he lost his seat in Parliament in 1922, following a disastrous campaign on the Conservative ticket in a working-class town.

Churchill remained out of Parliament until 1924. During this period he wrote numerous articles and produced a huge work that eventually filled six volumes and earned him a large profit. The book, called *The World Crisis*, was part autobiography and part history of the war.

Demanding regular work and an end to their dependence on welfare, British veterans parade through the streets of London shortly after the end of World War I. Their disillusionment with Britain's traditional political parties persuaded increasing numbers of working-class voters to support the Labour party.

Stanley Baldwin (1867–1947) was widely criticized for appointing Churchill to run the Treasury in 1924. Eventually, even Churchill decided that he had been a bad choice. "Everyone said I was the worst Chancellor of the Exchequer that ever was," he wrote late in his life, "and now I am inclined to agree with them."

63

Welsh coal miners join the 1926 general strike in which 6 million Britons walked off their jobs. Editing an emergency newspaper at the government's request, Churchill cheerfully dismissed accusations that his strike coverage was biased. "I decline utterly," he said, "to be impartial between the fire brigade and the fire."

> *Just try the process of outlining to Churchill a view with which he does not agree. You will find restive movements developing into mutterings, mutterings developing into thunderclaps and thunderclaps finally being followed by a torrential rain of argument in which your poor little view is utterly swamped.*
> —COLIN COOTE
> British journalist

When the Conservative politician Stanley Baldwin, a convinced trade protectionist, became prime minister in 1923, Churchill was inspired to consider seeking reelection as a Liberal who believed in free trade. Having made unsuccessful tries as a Liberal, he finally gained a seat in Parliament after proclaiming himself a "constitutionalist." He had, however, been eagerly adopted by Conservatives in the constituency he was running for since he only disagreed with them on economic issues. Prime Minister Baldwin recognized Churchill's value to the party and offered him a cabinet post as Chancellor of the Exchequer.

Churchill had little talent for this job. Managing the economy required flexibility, restraint, and a statistician's way of thinking. Churchill possessed none of these qualities. Some of his monetary policies were disastrous, and unemployment remained extremely high. Amid this discontent, in 1926, a government decision to sanction wage cuts in order to increase industrial efficiency provoked a strike by Britain's coal miners. This action erupted into a general strike of workers across the nation.

Churchill was furious. He accused the strikers of holding the country to ransom and vowed to do everything he could to defeat them. In cabinet meetings he declared his conviction that the government should not negotiate with the strikers. This was not the same Churchill who had calmly handled the strikes in the Welsh coal fields during his tenure at the Home Office. Churchill actually had no quarrel with the striking miners; he understood their grievances, and thought their action legitimate. The general strike, however, he considered a "concerted, deliberate organized menace." The strike eventually collapsed, shattered by the unwillingness of the government to compromise. The divisions in British society had grown wider than ever.

Churchill's views became increasingly conservative. By 1929 he was taking many old-fashioned positions and fighting against the tide of change. When the government proposed a bill to grant self-government to India, then a British colony, Churchill bitterly opposed it. Everyone knew it would be only a matter of time before India gained independence and few agreed with Churchill, who refused even to contemplate the possibility. When, in 1931, Prime Minister Baldwin accepted Indian independence in principle, Churchill resigned from the cabinet.

For the second time in 10 years, Churchill found himself isolated, alone in the political wilderness. People thought of him as a man embittered by his failure to realize his hopes and visions. It looked as though the 57-year-old Churchill, now consigned to the back benches of Parliament, was finished.

Yet Churchill himself, while not happy with the situation, managed to accept his lot. He knew there was still important work to be done.

For eight years, Churchill lived and worked as a political outcast. Because of his profoundly conservative views, and the extreme conviction with which he held them, he was distrusted by almost everyone in high government circles, even the leaders of the Conservative party. While he once had great influence, now no one listened, and the isolation pained him.

Once again Churchill devoted himself to his writing, which had always given him solace. At a time

> *I am not against the working man, but I implore him not to go down the wrong avenue seeking a paradise that is not there.*
> —DAVID LLOYD GEORGE voicing his fears that ordinary Britons would demand a socialist society, 1922

A mounted policeman attacks demonstrators in Bombay, India. Absolutely convinced that India should remain within the British Empire, Churchill refused to discuss independence with its leaders. "I am quite satisfied with my views on India," he said, "and I don't want them disturbed by any bloody Indians."

> *Either the Parliamentary institutions will emerge triumphant or the existing constitution will be fatally injured, and, however unwilling honourable members opposite may be to produce that result, the consequences of their action will inevitably lead to the erection of some Soviet of trade unions on which the real effective control of the economic and political life of the country will devolve.*
>
> —WINSTON CHURCHILL
> speaking during the general strike, May 3, 1926

when he no longer held the reins of power, he made his presence felt through the medium of the pen.

After completing the sixth and final volume of *The World Crisis*, his history of World War I (which one critic called Churchill's "autobiography disguised as a history of the universe"), he went on to write biographical pieces on the many powerful political figures he had known. These books were highly praised, widely read, and brought Churchill the money he needed to maintain his slightly extravagant lifestyle. His next project was extremely substantial. *Marlborough*, a biography of his ancestor, the first duke of Marlborough, was his major literary work of the 1930s. Churchill's command of language was considered brilliant, and he had become one of the world's most highly paid writers.

During this time, Churchill had many articles published in magazines and gave many speeches about the issues of the day. Not surprisingly, he always seemed to take the view that would prove least popular with the majority of his audience. In

Mohandas K. Gandhi (1869–1948), leader of the Indian independence movement, disembarks in England for a conference with British officials in 1931. An advocate of "passive resistance" rather than violence, Gandhi lived to see the end of British rule in India in 1947, but was assassinated by a fanatic a year later.

1936, when King George V died, his son, the prince of Wales, became Kind Edward VIII. His accession to the throne, however, did not deflect him from his intention to marry American socialite Wallis Simpson, who was then in the process of divorcing her second husband. The British were in an uproar over the impending marriage of their king to someone who was both a commoner and a double divorcée. The government strongly opposed it. Churchill took the romantic view. He thought the king should be able to marry anyone he wanted, and he was joined in his sentiments by such unlikely figures as Oswald Mosley, leader of the British Union of Fascists, and George Bernard Shaw, the leading playwright and left-wing political commentator. Government opposition, however, carried the day. Edward abdicated and his younger brother became King George VI.

It was foreign affairs, however, that particularly absorbed Churchill during the 1930s. A lifelong student of history and the ways of nations, Churchill saw the dangers brewing in Europe long be-

> *Now the demand is that Germany should be allowed to rearm. . . . Do not let His Majesty's Government believe that all that Germany is asking for is equal status. . . . All these bands of sturdy Teutonic youths, marching through the streets and roads of Germany, with the light of desire in their eyes to suffer for their Fatherland, when they have the weapons, believe me they will ask for the return of lost territories and lost colonies.*
> —WINSTON CHURCHILL
> speaking in the House of Commons on November 23, 1932

Sir Oswald Mosley (1896–1980), leader of the British Union of Fascists, returns the salutes of his followers during a 1937 march through London. Churchill had no use for Mosley—he called the wealthy extremist a "gilded butterfly"—or his organization, whose members approved of the fascist governments that had been in power in Italy since 1922 and in Germany since 1933.

Churchill became aware of the threat to peace that Adolf Hitler (1889–1945) represented long before the German fascist's accession to the chancellorship in 1933. The Nazi (National Socialist) leader saw the Briton in the very same light. He called Churchill a *Deutschenfresser* ("devourer of Germans").

fore the majority of his countrymen. The speeches of the new German chancellor, Adolf Hitler, who came to power in 1933, greatly disturbed Churchill. Hitler was declaring that the Germans were the "master race," and that they would avenge "all [the] wrongs done to [them] by the Jews." (Hitler and his followers believed that Germany's defeat in World War I had been caused by the machinations of communist subversives and Jewish financiers on the home front.)

Churchill began to speak out about the dark and ominous implications of Hitler's words. Few people listened, however. Pointing to the fact that Germany had begun to expand its armed forces way beyond the 100,000-man limit dictated by the Allies in the negotiations conducted at Versailles in 1919, Churchill urged the British government to begin a massive rearmament programme immediately.

In March 1936 Hitler took the first step in what was to prove a policy of expansion. His armies moved into the Rhineland, a section of western Germany that the Allies had ordered demilitarized after World War I. Even though Churchill's predictions were proving correct, still they were ignored. The next year Hitler unfolded his master plan. In an address to senior army commanders he declared that Germany needed *Lebensraum* (living space) and that such territorial expansion was to be achieved by the forceful occupation of large areas of eastern Europe. This action would entail the enslavement of the inhabitants in the areas invaded. Just three years after this speech Hitler was to establish a new and even more terrible policy linked to the expansionist adventures—the notorious "final solution" to what he called "the Jewish question." Not just Germany's Jews but those living in eastern Europe and the Soviet Union, the areas he intended to take over, would be targeted for mass murder.

In 1938, when Hitler began to put pressure on Czechoslovakia, Britain's prime minister, Neville Chamberlain, remained convinced that war between his country and Germany could be averted. In keeping with the attitude of the majority of British politicians at that time, Chamberlain did not take Churchill's warnings seriously.

Chamberlain's foreign policy was, in fact, a perfect example of the political practise known as appeasement. This is a method of conducting foreign policy whereby one makes concessions to an enemy if doing so is the only alternative to war. Chamberlain had first revealed himself as an advocate of appeasement in 1936, when he allowed Nazi Germany to occupy the Rhineland. Then, in 1938, he failed to oppose Hitler when the dictator united Germany and Austria politically, even though it was forbidden under the terms of the Treaty of Versailles.

Chamberlain's attitude led him to make a tragic error of judgment that resulted in the act for which he is most remembered. Late in 1938 Hitler invited Chamberlain, along with French prime minister Edouard Daladier and Italian dictator Benito Mussolini, to attend a conference in Munich, Germany.

A Star of David identifies a streetcar reserved for Jewish use in Warsaw, Poland. Until World War II began, the Nazis limited their persecution of the Jews largely to confiscation of property, harassment, and isolation. Once the war started, however, Hitler embarked on a systematic campaign to kill every Jew in Europe.

During the talks Hitler declared that the only additional territory he wished to incorporate into Germany was a small part of Czechoslovakia, the predominantly German-speaking Sudetenland. The four men talked, and a statement was prepared in which Britain and France yielded to Hitler's demands. Chamberlain also got Hitler to co-sign a statement to the effect that Britain and Germany agreed never to go to war again.

Securing Hitler's signature on this document convinced Chamberlain that he had prevented a major war. Churchill, however, was outraged. He knew that Hitler's promises were worthless. The German dictator soon made a mockery of the Munich agreements, and in March 1939 his troops occupied the rest of Czechoslovakia, an event which came as the culmination of a diplomatic offensive that had disestablished Czechoslovakia as a unified and sovereign state.

It is generally agreed by historians that it was Hitler's occupation of Czechoslovakia that forced Chamberlain to abandon appeasement. Faced with this last example of Hitler's perfidy, Britain and France replaced appeasement with a policy of "guarantees." They promised to aid Romania, Greece, and Poland should any of these countries be attacked. It was not long before the guarantees were put to the test.

During the summer of 1939 Germany began to demand territorial concessions from Poland. Hitler wanted various sections of the country that had belonged to Germany until 1919, when the victorious Allies had redrawn the defeated nation's borders at Versailles. Chamberlain finally stopped accommodating Hitlerite expansionism when Germany and the Soviet Union signed a nonaggression treaty on August 23, 1939. Hitler could now attack Poland, secure in the knowledge that the Soviet Union would not intervene. (In fact, under the terms of this treaty, the Soviet Union and Germany had agreed to divide Poland between them.) Later that same day Britain and Poland contracted a formal alliance. On September 1, 1939, German troops and armour thundered into Poland.

Neville Chamberlain (1869–1940), who served as prime minister from 1937 to 1940, came under much criticism from Churchill for his failure to object to the expansionist foreign policy that Hitlerite Germany was pursuing at the expense of Britain's European allies.

British Prime Minister Neville Chamberlain visits Italian dictator Benito Mussolini (right; 1883–1945) in 1939. Chamberlain had been applauded as a hero by his countrymen after an earlier visit to Hitler. He had secured, he said with characteristic but unrealistic optimism, "peace with honour." Churchill disagreed emphatically. Chamberlain, he said, had secured "total . . . defeat."

Chamberlain called for Churchill immediately. Public demand for Churchill's inclusion in a wartime government had grown loud and insistent. Chamberlain knew that he could no longer afford to do without Churchill and offered him a place in the war cabinet. On September 2 Britain issued an ultimatum to Germany demanding that its forces withdraw from Poland. When the deadline expired at 11:00 A.M. on September 3, Neville Chamberlain announced to the British people that a state of war now existed between their country and Germany. Later that day Churchill was appointed First Lord of the Admiralty and the signal went out to the British fleet: "Winston is back."

Poland's antiquated armed forces crumbled before the German onslaught and organized resistance finally ceased on October 5.

Warsaw's Jews — men, women, and children — are marched off to concentration camps by German troops. The Germans had set the Warsaw ghetto on fire after its desperate, poorly armed residents had tried to resist deportation to the camps, where they would face certain death.

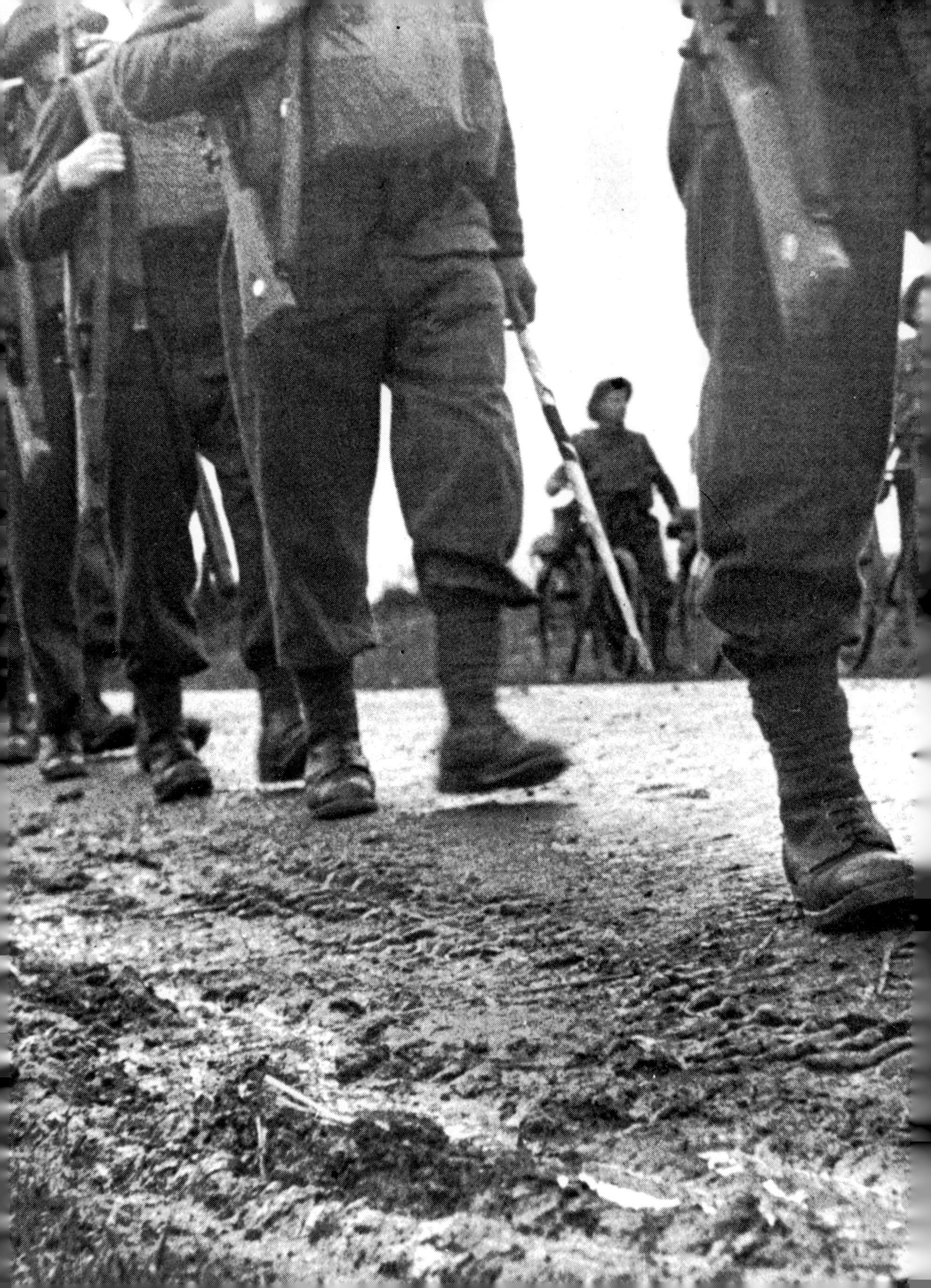

6

The Warlord

> *Never in the field of human conflict was so much owed by so many to so few.*
> —WINSTON CHURCHILL speaking in tribute to the Royal Air Force on August 20, 1940

In April 1940 German forces occupied Denmark and Norway as a prelude to a major offensive in the west. Hitler's armies prepared for action on a front that stretched from the Netherlands to northeastern France. Once again France was destined to be the theatre of brutal fighting, and Hitler had decided to take advantage of the two weakest elements in that country's defensive capability. His intended victim was not the same nation that had thrown itself into battle with such suicidal valour in 1914. France had lost 1.35 million young men in that war, and the country's fighting spirit had suffered irreparable damage. Equally as dangerous as this lack of morale was the fact that French military planners still believed that France was adequately protected by the Maginot Line, a system of fortifications along the Franco-German border. Built between 1929 and 1934, the system had failed to extend along the Franco-Belgian border due to cost overruns. As a result, France remained extremely vulnerable on its northern border.

The Allied failure to eject the Germans from Norway had greatly disturbed the British public. People were shocked at the incompetence of the country's military and civilian leadership.

In the early hours of May 10, 1940, German forces invaded the Netherlands, Belgium, and Luxembourg. Chamberlain and his policy of appease-

Churchill's energy and optimism were credited with inspiring his countrymen's gritty determination to resist Hitler's onslaughts. With uncharacteristic modesty, however, he said that the "British race" had the heart of a lion, and that he had merely been "called upon to give the roar."

For six long, weary years the ground of Europe shook under the ceaseless pounding of millions of boots. World War II, fought from 1939 to 1945, cost the lives of 14 million soldiers and uncountable numbers of civilians all over the globe.

73

France's Maginot Line — a string of border forts designed to stop invading forces — probably seemed as curiously outdated during the 1930s as it does to contemporary eyes. Military historians, however, believe it might have worked if it had not ended in northeastern France, thus allowing German armoured divisions to attack across the Franco-Belgian border.

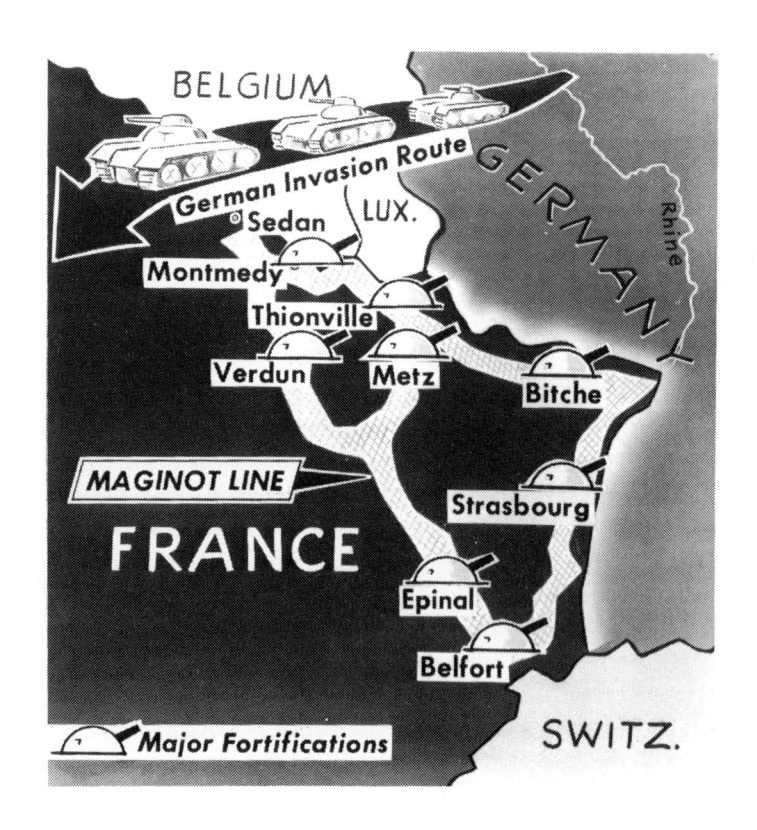

ment now stood discredited as never before, and there was no doubt among the men who walked the corridors of power in Britain that Chamberlain was finished. The prime minister knew that he could no longer govern the nation effectively and lead it through war. The Labour party leaders made it known that Churchill was the only possible Conservative prime minister with whom they would consider working in a wartime coalition government. That same evening, Churchill received the royal assent to his appointment from King George VI. Winston Churchill was now prime minister of Great Britain.

For the ever-gallant Churchill there could have been no greater honour than to lead his country through times of crisis. In fact, his enormous responsibilities came as a relief to him. Now he was free to get things done the way he thought they should be done. The task that lay before him was truly formidable.

On the same day that he took office as prime minister, Churchill appeared before the House of Commons and delivered what was to become one of his most famous speeches. "I have nothing to offer but blood, toil, tears, and sweat," he told Parliament. "You ask, What is our aim? I can answer in one word: victory—victory in spite of all terror; victory, however long and hard the road may be; for without victory there is no survival." His words received the unanimous support of all who heard them.

On June 13, 1940, as British and French troops marched northward to relieve the pressure on Belgium (where they still imagined the decisive battles would be fought) events took an unexpected turn for the worse in northeastern France.

German armour crossed the Meuse River at Sedan (where the Allied commanders had least expected such an attack) and began to drive hard and fast across northern France. The Germans planned to cut off the predominantly British forces in Belgium (who were already suffering heavy casualties) from further reinforcement by the French. They succeeded brilliantly. The British fell back before this onslaught from two directions and were forced to conduct a fighting retreat to the French coast. Evacuating from the port of Dunkirk, under constant attack from German aircraft and leaving most of their equipment behind, the British forces barely succeeded in escaping annihilation.

> . . . *if we fail, then the whole world, including the United States, including all that we have known and cared for, will sink into the abyss of a new dark age made more sinister, and perhaps more protracted, by the lights of perverted science. Let us therefore brace ourselves to our duties, and so bear ourselves that, if the British Empire and its Commonwealth last for a thousand years, men will still say, 'This was their finest hour.'*
> —WINSTON CHURCHILL speaking in the House of Commons on June 18, 1940

Despite relentless German aerial and artillery bombardment, the retreating British forces managed to evacuate 338,000 men from the French port of Dunkirk in June 1940. Aiding the Royal Navy in this astonishing feat were hundreds of civilians — fishermen, yachtsmen, and fireboat crews — who courageously crossed the English Channel in small boats to help rescue both English and French soldiers.

Royal Air Force pilots sprint for their planes as enemy bombers approach in 1940. Although the German air force was superior in numbers, the RAF fought it to a standstill. "Never," said Churchill, of Britain's debt to its flyers, "has so much been owed by so many to so few."

The effect of this withdrawal upon the French was disastrous. Their entire command structure had fallen apart, and the end was in sight. On June 22, 1940, the French government agreed to an armistice and Britain found itself facing the Hitlerite threat alone.

Just a few days after the French surrender, Churchill had to make one of the toughest decisions of his entire career. The French fleet in the Mediterranean was now controlled by the régime that the Germans had installed in those parts of France that were not directly occupied by Germany. Led by World War I hero Henri Philippe Pétain, this collaborationist and violently anti-British government established a policy of effective neutrality. Though the Germans had guaranteed not to seize the French fleet, many British military and civilian leaders believed that they would eventually renege on the promise. And the French fleet contained many large ships that would be a major threat to the British navy if they were ever to sail under the German flag.

Accordingly, on July 3, 1940, a British squadron attacked French warships at anchor in the Algerian port of Mers-el-Kebir. Over 1,500 French sailors died. The massacre greatly disturbed those among their compatriots who had fled to Britain after the fall of France rather than live under German occupation or the collaborationists.

It was a perilous time for Britain, and many neutral observers thought its survival impossible.

Hitler was predicting an early end to the war, claiming that he would overrun Britain just as easily as he had overwhelmed France. But he had not counted on the determination of the British people and their new leader.

Thanks to Churchill's rousing speeches, the British fighting spirit was never stronger. He regularly addressed the nation by means of radio broadcasts. After the fall of France, Churchill stressed repeatedly that nothing less than total victory would do. In one of his best-remembered speeches, delivered shortly after the Dunkirk disaster, he said, "Even though large tracts of Europe and many old and famous States have fallen into the grip of . . . all the odious apparatus of Nazi rule, we shall not flag or fail. We shall go on to the end. We shall fight in France, we shall fight on the seas and oceans, we shall fight with growing confidence and growing strength in the air, we shall defend our island, whatever the cost may be." Churchill's inspiring speeches came to be considered some of the greatest orations of all time.

In July 1940 the German air force commenced bombing operations against British shipping in the Channel. The British struck back, and the Battle of Britain—the first major strategic air war in history—began.

Britain's Royal Air Force was comparatively new and largely untested. During the previous 20 years it had mainly been employed abroad, conducting policing operations on the borders of Britain's far-flung imperial territories. The majority of its pilots were young and completely untried in aerial combat. During the 1930s, Churchill had continually implored the government to take note of the extent to which Germany was rebuilding its air force. But his had been a voice in the wilderness. German pilots had gained combat experience between 1936 and 1939 fighting in the Spanish Civil War on the side of General Francisco Franco's fascists. The British people, however, were treated to the far from reassuring sight of the Royal Air Force's antiquated and lumbering biplanes going through their aerobatic motions at countless air shows. The Brit-

Spanish head of state Francisco Franco (1892–1975) with his wife and daughter in the 1930s. The Spanish Civil War (1936–1939) served as a "dress rehearsal" for World War II, with Hitler and Mussolini supporting Franco's fascist rebels and the Soviet Union aiding the forces loyal to the elected government. Franco won, but he kept his nation neutral during the global conflict that followed.

Hermann Göring (1893–1946), a longtime supporter of Hitler, was responsible for creating and commanding the *Luftwaffe* (Nazi Germany's air force). He told Hitler that his planes could destroy both the Royal Navy and the RAF, thus ensuring a successful invasion of England. Events proved him to have been overconfident.

ish government did eventually begin production of modern aircraft toward the end of the 1930s. Despite Churchill's warnings, however, Britain's airmen faced a desperate situation in the summer of 1940.

At the beginning of the battle the Germans had a distinct numerical advantage in terms both of pilots and aircraft. But they were not to meet with the easy victory that they had anticipated. Hermann Göring, the German air force chief, refused to rotate his crews due to his conviction that a quick victory was certain. Göring's failure to compromise on his original decision once it became apparent that he had been overly optimistic was to affect German operational efficiency and morale very seriously indeed.

The technological superiority of the most up-to-date British fighter, the Spitfire, combined with the RAF's embryonic radar-guided interception capability, eventually proved decisive. The RAF fought a sober and careful battle of attrition, successfully stemming the German tide.

Hitler then ordered Göring to switch from operations against RAF airfields and to direct his raids against London and other important British cities. He hoped thus to break the spirit of Britain's civilian population. This allowed the RAF a respite from constant combat and gave it time in which to repair its airfields and regroup. Even though for several months as many as 300 German bombers attacked London on a daily basis, Britain's air marshals were able to breathe a sigh of relief. They knew that as long as the airfields remained serviceable, the Royal Air Force could keep flying.

At about this time, Churchill began to turn to another ally for help. So far, the Americans had remained neutral, but their sympathies were with Britain and the fight against Hitler. The United States, under the leadership of President Franklin D. Roosevelt, agreed to support the British war effort by making all kinds of military equipment available under the terms of the Lend-Lease Bill, which became law on March 11, 1941.

The warships and merchant vessels that Britain

A German pilot's-eye view of an RAF Spitfire fighter plane during a World War II air battle. Sure that his bombers would bring Britain to its knees, Hitler offered peace terms in 1940. "I do not propose," responded Churchill, "to reply to Herr Hitler's speech, not being on speaking terms with him."

obtained on the Lend-Lease account greatly aided the nation's effort in a fierce and desperate war at sea. The nation's lifeline was at stake. Many shiploads of desperately needed food and supplies were sunk by German submarines. The British navy, which had traditionally enjoyed absolute supremacy at sea, suffered severe losses in the course of escorting convoys back and forth across the Atlantic.

In July 1941, shortly after the German invasion of the Soviet Union, cooperation between the United States and Britain became even closer. Churchill met with President Roosevelt, and the two men laid down guidelines for the coordination of production, logistical, and intelligence efforts. They also issued a joint declaration that became known as the Atlantic Charter. In this statement both leaders expressed their commitment to democracy and to world prosperity and advocated "the abandonment of the use of force." As the Royal Navy continued its efforts to keep the Atlantic open to British shipping, there was also heavy fighting in North Africa, where the British faced German armoured and infantry forces led by a brilliant young general named Erwin Rommel.

When, in June 1941, Hitler's armies invaded the Soviet Union, Churchill began to see some light at the end of the tunnel. His enemy would now be fighting on two fronts, and Churchill believed that Germany had signed its own death warrant by taking this dangerous and ill-conceived step. The German invasion took the Soviets almost completely by surprise and their losses were horrifying. Jo-

> *I cannot conceal from the reader of this truthful account that as I went to bed at about 3 a.m., I was conscious of a profound sense of relief. At last I had the authority to give directions over the whole scene. I felt as if I were walking with Destiny, and that all my past life had been but a preparation for this hour and for this trial. . . . I thought I knew a good deal about it all, and I was sure I should not fail.*
> —WINSTON CHURCHILL writing about his appointment as prime minister on May 10, 1940

> *Here is the answer which I give to President Roosevelt: Put your confidence in us. . . . We shall not fail or falter; we shall not weaken or tire. Neither the sudden shock of battle, nor the long-drawn trials of vigilance and exertion will wear us down. Give us the tools and we will finish the job.*
>
> —WINSTON CHURCHILL
> in a radio address delivered on February 9, 1941, requesting material assistance from the United States

seph Stalin, the Soviet dictator, begged Britain and the United States to help his country by sending as much military equipment as possible. Churchill and Roosevelt, despite their dislike of the communist system of government, agreed to the Soviet request. By the end of 1941 the Red Army had begun to recover from its early shattering defeats, and senior Soviet commanders were planning their first major counteroffensive.

Britain and the United States became formal allies in December 1941. American opposition to Japan's expansionist policies had angered the government in Tokyo, and many observers had long foreseen the possibility of conflict between the two nations. On December 7, 1941, Japanese naval aircraft attacked elements of the U.S. Pacific fleet at Pearl Harbour in Hawaii. Germany and Italy then declared war on the United States just four days later. Roosevelt, against much domestic opposition, firmly believed that the main Allied effort should be directed against Germany. Later that same month Churchill accordingly informed Roosevelt of his plan to open a front in North Africa, where British forces had so far failed to gain the upper hand in the battle against Rommel.

Churchill was eager to secure a victory in North Africa and then to invade Sicily and press on into Italy from the south. This move, he felt, would secure Allied communications in the Mediterranean, dilute the German effort against the hard-pressed Soviets, and intensify the pressure on Italy.

Churchill was sure that Allied victories in North Africa would help decisively to tip the scales against Hitler. At first, the Allies suffered considerable losses in North Africa, since the Germans, although at a numerical disadvantage, continued to fight with remarkable skill and flexibility. Finally, under the leadership of America's General Dwight D. Eisenhower, Allied forces took the offensive against enemy units in western North Africa. This action occurred shortly after the commencement of the British Eighth Army's crushing assault on the German forces at Alamein in eastern North Africa in October and November of 1942. By February 1943 the bulk of Italian and German forces in North Africa had surrendered.

In January 1943 Churchill conferred with President Roosevelt at Casablanca in French Morocco. The Americans pressed for an Allied invasion of France as soon as possible, but Churchill insisted on the need for a concentration of effort in the Mediterranean theatre. Roosevelt finally agreed in principle to the idea of an Allied invasion of Italy and the postponement of action against the Germans in northern France. This decision did not particularly please the Soviets, who rightly believed that nothing but an Allied invasion of northern Europe would substantially reduce German pressure on the Soviet Union. As things turned out, German resistance in Italy was much stiffer than the Allied commanders had anticipated, and the campaigns there proved both costly and protracted.

German strength in general, however, was starting to reach its limits. On December 6, 1943, President Roosevelt informed Churchill that he had

Churchill inspects bomb damage in London in 1941. Disregarding his advisers, he often appeared on the city's streets during the incessant bombing known as the Blitz, and he called "unthinkable" a proposal that the government move out of London.

> *Winston never had the slightest doubt that he had inherited all the military genius of his great ancestor, Marlborough. His military plans and ideas varied from the most brilliant conceptions at the one end to the wildest and most dangerous ideas at the other. To wean him away from these wilder plans required superhuman efforts and was never entirely successful in so far as he tended to return to these again and again.*
> —GENERAL SIR ALAN BROOKE

appointed General Eisenhower supreme Allied commander for Operation Overlord—the invasion of northern Europe. The invasion was set for May or June of 1944.

The assault on the beaches at Normandy in northwestern France took place on D-Day—June 6, 1944. The Allies had taken advantage of a forecast that promised a 36-hour break in the otherwise poor weather. The Germans, however, had believed that the bad weather would persist and that there would be no Allied landings for some time.

The invasion began at dawn, and took the Germans by surprise. Hitler's troops, although outnumbered, fought back with great determination. Although D-Day was undoubtedly the beginning of the end for the Germans in western Europe, the war was far from over. The battle-hardened Nazis conducted a stubborn fighting retreat, inflicting terrible casualties on their opponents, many of whom lacked combat experience. However, the German position in France finally began to collapse when American forces under General Omar Bradley effected a major breakthrough in the region of St. Lô at the end of July 1944. This action left thousands of German troops stranded in the Cherbourg peninsula, cut off from their supply bases to the east.

By mid-August Allied armoured formations had fought their way through to open country and were racing across northern France. On August 25 General Charles de Gaulle, leader of the Free French forces, made a triumphant entry into Paris. The arrival of this remarkable soldier and patriot in the capital of the country he loved so dearly marked the culmination of his wartime career as chief of the French forces in exile. The relationship between Churchill and de Gaulle had often been stormy. President Roosevelt disliked the Frenchman, and Churchill had on many occasions no choice but to favour American decisions. In de Gaulle's opinion, these decisions failed to take sufficient account of French interests. De Gaulle had never forgiven Roosevelt for continuing to recognize the Pétain government.

In the wake of these successes, the Allied advance into Europe ran into serious trouble in September 1944. General Eisenhower decided to mount an airborne operation across the Rhine River and thus take the war into the heart of Germany. This ambitious attempt to deliver a blow that would force the Germans to capitulate did not succeed. The lightly armed British and American paratroops found themselves facing German armoured divisions

Respected by both sides for the tactical cunning he displayed in North Africa, Field-Marshal Erwin Rommel (left; 1891–1944), commander of the famed *Afrika Korps*, was admiringly known as "the Desert Fox." He committed suicide after Hitler's secret police discovered that he was implicated in a plot to assassinate Hitler.

The "day of infamy" — December 7, 1941 — when Japanese planes rained bombs on the American fleet at Pearl Harbour, marked the entrance of the United States into World War II. The surprise raid killed 2,400 Americans and knocked out 18 warships and 347 planes.

that were refitting in the drop-zones. The combination of this disadvantage and the fact that bad weather was hampering the reinforcements moving up from the south created a military disaster for the Allies. Barely a quarter of the original airborne force made it back across the Rhine following the decision to evacuate.

In mid-December 1944 the Allies received another shock when the Germans staged a completely unanticipated offensive in the west. Hitler had transferred many divisions from the eastern front in order to mount this counterattack in the Ardennes region of northern France, and his men made astonishing progress for several days, protected from Allied ground-attack aircraft by seasonal fog and low cloud. Thousands of Allied troops surrendered before the German onslaught. The engagement became known as the Battle of the Bulge due to the fact that the German forces quickly fanned out after their initial breakthrough, thus creating a huge balloonlike indentation in the Allied front. Eisenhower and his senior commanders were not quite sure what had hit them at first, but they began to retrieve the situation early in January 1945, taking advantage of the fact that by then the German advance had slowed to a crawl due to fuel shortages and stiffening Allied resistance. The situation became even more desperate for the Germans when the first breaks in the weather enabled the Allies to unleash their overwhelming airpower. The slaughter was appalling. The Germans had no air cover of their own and nowhere to run. Hitler's last desperate gamble to force the western Allies to negotiate had failed.

By January 1945 it had become apparent that the Red Army would be hammering at the outskirts of Berlin long before the British and Americans had advanced very far into Germany. In February Churchill met with Roosevelt and Stalin at Yalta, a resort town on the shores of the Black Sea. Despite the fact that at this conference Stalin hailed Winston as "the man who is born once in a hundred years" and "the bravest statesman in the world," the Soviet dictator knew that the Red Army's

Participants in the 1943 Casablanca Conference. It was at this meeting that the Allies decided to accept nothing less than the unconditional surrender of Germany, Italy, and Japan.

> *On my right sat the President of the United States, on my left the Master of Russia. Together we controlled practically all the naval and three-quarters of all the air forces in the world, and could direct armies of nearly twenty millions of men, engaged in the most terrible of wars that had yet occurred in human history.*
> —WINSTON CHURCHILL
> writing about his meeting with Roosevelt and Stalin at Teheran in 1943

runaway successes in eastern Europe had effectively made Churchill and Roosevelt only junior partners in the drive into Germany.

Churchill, exhibiting his habitual political astuteness, hedged his bets with regard to just what had really been achieved by the talks. He had, he said, the impression "that Marshal Stalin and the Soviet leaders wish to live in honourable friendship and equality with the western democracies. . . . I decline absolutely to embark here on a discussion about Russian good faith. . . . Sombre indeed would be the fortunes of mankind if some awful schism arose between the western democracies and the Soviet Union."

His problems became even more severe when the ailing President Roosevelt died of a cerebral haemorrhage at Warm Springs, Georgia, on April 12, 1945. The United States had lost an outstanding leader and Churchill found himself deprived of a much-valued associate upon whom he had come increasingly to depend. In an address to the House of Commons he paid tribute to Franklin Delano Roosevelt as "the greatest American friend we have ever known, and the greatest champion of freedom who has ever brought help and comfort from the new world to the old."

General Dwight D. Eisenhower (1890–1969) briefs paratroopers before the invasion of France in June 1944. The general—known to friend and foe as "Ike"—planned and commanded the invasion of Nazi-occupied western Europe. He served as U.S. president from 1953 to 1961.

Within days of Roosevelt's death the war in Europe ground to a halt. Several months of ferocious strategic bombing had finally destroyed Germany's capacity to produce oil. The country's transport system was immobilized and its industries were utterly wrecked.

Adolf Hitler committed suicide in his bunker beneath the ruins of Berlin on April 30, 1945. On May 8 General Eisenhower received the unconditional surrender of all German forces in a ceremony at his headquarters in the French city of Reims. The war in Europe was over.

With the securing of victory in Europe Churchill was soon to find himself in a quite unprecedented position. It was Churchill the great wartime leader that people hailed, not Churchill the political leader. Churchill had failed to comprehend the extent to which war-weary Britons felt the need for a radical change of direction. As he rode through the streets of London amid cheering crowds, Churchill was largely ignorant of the fact that new, progressive sentiments had begun to pervade British society. Elections were to be held, and Churchill, the Conservative prime minister, would, in effect, be requesting a mandate to finish his country's business with Japan as he saw fit.

Operation Overlord begins as Allied soldiers struggle away from their landing craft and wade ashore in France on D-Day — June 6, 1944. D-Day witnessed the largest airborne attack in history: 183,000 paratroopers and 1,000 aeroplanes. Thousands of Allied troops died on the beaches, but the invasion succeeded, bringing into view the end of Hitler's European empire.

"The Big Three"—Churchill, Roosevelt, and Soviet leader Joseph V. Stalin (1879–1953)—meet at Yalta in 1945. Neither Churchill nor Roosevelt trusted "Uncle Joe" Stalin (who had once said, "sincere diplomacy is no more possible than dry water"), but they were encouraged by his promise to declare war on Japan once Germany surrendered.

In July, Churchill attended a conference at Potsdam, Germany. There he met with Joseph Stalin and Franklin Roosevelt's successor, President Truman. The three men discussed both the prosecution of the war against Japan and, equally if not more important, the political shape of the postwar world. The bargaining at these talks was extremely hard, and it was there that Churchill learned that the Americans had been successful in their protracted and phenomenally expensive efforts to produce an atomic bomb. Churchill had no illusions as to the implications of this terrifying new weapon. He wrote: "We seemed suddenly to have become possessed of a merciful abridgment of the slaughter in the East and of a far happier prospect in Europe. I have no doubt that these thoughts were present in the minds of my American friends. At any rate, there never was a moment's discussion as to whether the atomic bomb should be used or not. To avert a vast, indefinite butchery, to bring the war to an end, to give peace to the world, to lay healing hands upon its tortured peoples by a manifestation of overwhelming power at the cost of a few explosions, seemed, after all our toils and perils, a miracle of deliverance."

On July 25, 1945, Churchill returned to Britain to await the results of the election. That morning he had awoken in a state of extreme depression, as if sensing that further difficulties lay ahead. The hardening of attitudes that had characterized the Potsdam talks seemed somehow ominous. Six years of war had changed the world beyond recognition: the Soviets now stood astride vast tracts of eastern Europe; Britain had emerged as something of a junior partner in the wartime alliance; and President Truman, almost unnoticed, had effectively reserved to himself a right of veto on all the agreements reached at the conference.

In his memoirs Churchill gives an account of the dream from which he had awoken that morning: "I dreamed that life was over. I saw—it was very

American sailors and British civilians—like millions of others all over the world—celebrate the news that Germany has surrendered at last. Addressing a huge London crowd on May 8, 1945, Churchill said, "This is your victory."

vivid—my dead body under a white sheet on a table in an empty room. I recognized my bare feet projecting from under the sheet. It was very lifelike. . . . Perhaps this is the end."

On July 26, as the early returns began to come in, it became apparent that the Conservatives were losing. (Some historians have estimated that as many as 80% of British servicemen voted against Churchill and the Conservatives in this election, hoping perhaps that a Labour government would create the "Land Fit for Heroes" that Lloyd George and the Liberals had promised and then conspicuously failed to deliver at the end of World War I.) By midday the fact of an overwhelming Labour victory was beyond dispute and the only consolation for Churchill was that he had retained his own seat in Parliament and would thus become leader of the opposition.

Stunned by this defeat, Churchill shared his thoughts with his family and a few close friends later that day. He said, "The new government will have terrible tasks. Terrible tasks. We must do all we can to help them. . . . It will be strange tomorrow not to be consulted upon the great affairs of State."

There was still heavy fighting between the Allies and the Japanese in the Pacific. Allied commanders in that theatre knew that invading Japan could prove one of the costliest operations of the entire war. Their worst fears were never to be realized. President Truman made one of the toughest decisions ever taken by a 20th-century head of state and sanctioned the use of the atomic bomb against Japan. Hiroshima suffered atomic annihilation by a uranium-charged weapon on August 6, 1945, and Nagasaki was devastated by a bomb charged with plutonium, an even more deadly and powerful substance, on August 9.

Japan surrendered on August 14, helpless before this new American weaponry that was capable of causing unparalleled devastation.

Despite Churchill's account of the original reaction to the news that the bomb had been successfully tested, many Allied military and civilian leaders

President Harry S. Truman (1884–1972) shakes hands with Churchill and Stalin in Potsdam, Germany, in June 1945. Churchill established an immediate rapport with Truman, but he missed Roosevelt, who had died of a cerebral haemorrhage on April 12. He called the late president "the greatest American friend we have ever known."

had raised questions about the ethicality of deploying it. Admiral William D. Leahy, a top adviser to Truman, later expressed the opinion that the Americans had "adopted an ethical standard common to the barbarians of the Dark Ages."

Churchill too had expressed similar doubts in the wake of his initial enthusiasm. He wrote: "It would be a mistake to suppose that the fate of Japan was settled by the atomic bomb. Her defeat was certain before the first bomb fell, and was brought about by overwhelming maritime power. This alone had made it possible to seize ocean bases from which to launch the final attack and force her metropolitan Army to capitulate without striking a blow. Her shipping had been destroyed." These words of Churchill's seem almost to give credence to a statement made in 1984 by British historian Tariq Ali. He suggested that the American deployment of atomic bombs against Japan was really intended as a nuclear warning "shot across Stalin's bows."

Indeed, everything had changed. Britons had no

The first plutonium bomb, code-named "Fat Man," annihilated 74,800 people in Nagasaki on August 9, 1945. The Japanese had refused to give up after Hiroshima was bombed, but they cabled their acceptance in principle of the Allied terms of unconditional surrender less than 24 hours after the disaster at Nagasaki. The war ended four days later.

The pilot (centre) and ground crew of the *Enola Gay*, the American B-29 bomber that dropped an atom bomb on Hiroshima, Japan, on August 6, 1945. Equal in destructive power to 20,000 tons of TNT, the bomb killed 100,000 people instantly.

Many residents of Hiroshima, the Japanese city destroyed by an American atom bomb on August 6, 1945, suffered radiation poisoning and burns that rendered them unrecognizable; 100,000 of those people who had survived died the following year. People who had been within 1,000 yards of the bomb's detonation point simply evaporated, leaving their shadows permanently imprinted on streets and the walls of buildings.

illusions about the reduced role their country would play in the postwar world, and Churchill realized that a global order built upon the foundations of the decisions and intrigues of Potsdam would bear little resemblance to the one he had known during his many years of public service. Faced with the election of a socialist government in Britain and the fact that the most important decisions about the world's affairs would now be taken in Moscow and Washington, Churchill stated that the British "had had very early and increasingly to recognize the limitations of our own power and influence, great though it be, in the gaunt world arising from the ruins of this hideous war."

> *A Churchill Cabinet was primarily an opportunity for the Prime Minister to tell his colleagues what was happening, what he thought about it, and how he meant to deal with it, followed by as much of the agenda as time allowed.*
> —LEO AMERY
> Conservative party M.P.

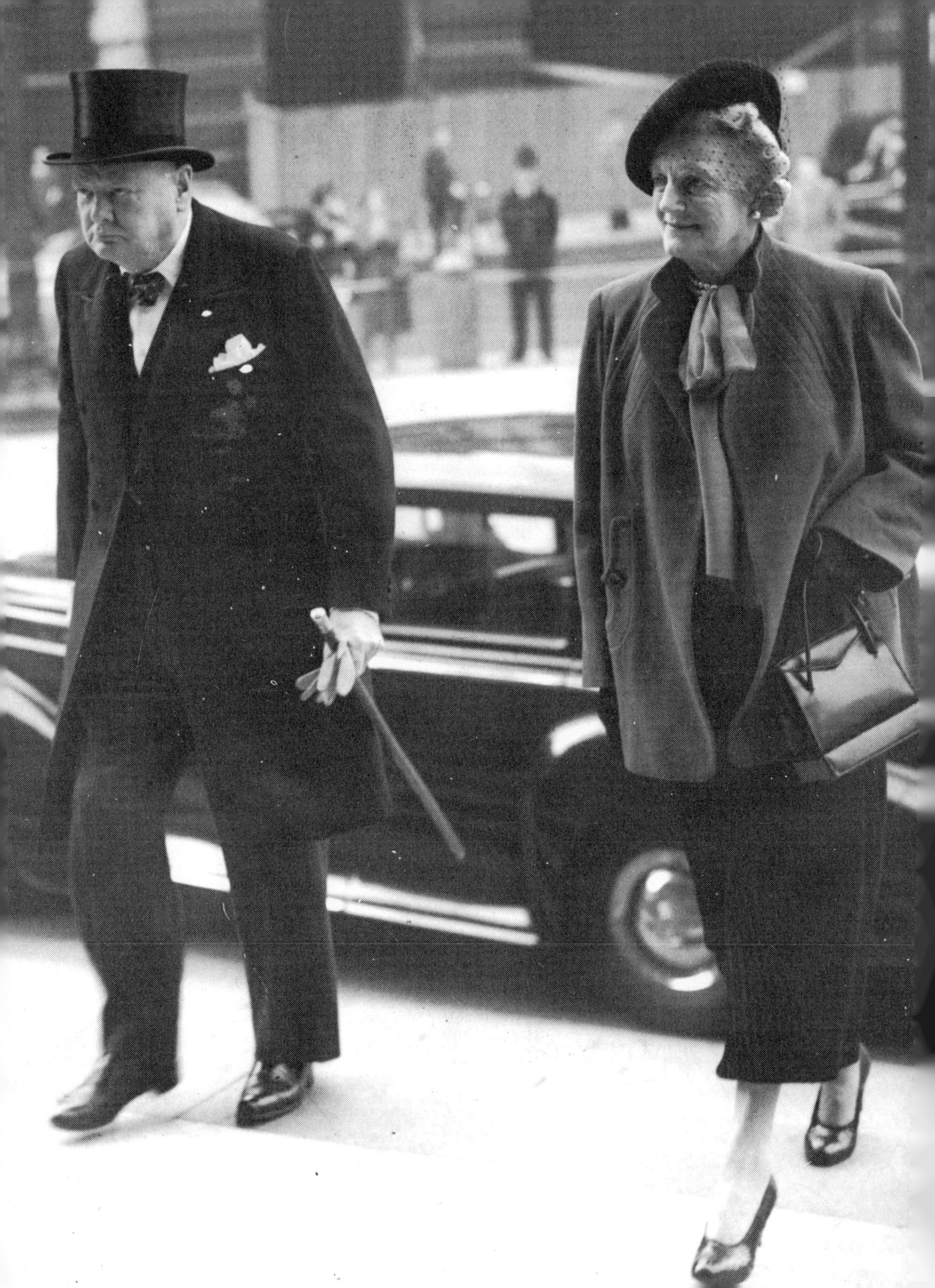

7

Confronting the Brave New World

News of the Conservatives' defeat spread around the globe, causing much consternation. Not only had Churchill fallen from power, but his socialist opponents had won by a landslide. The Labour party, full of young men with comparatively revolutionary ideas for rebuilding the country and remodelling British society, had finally come to power. Clement Attlee, who had led the Labour party since 1935, was the new prime minister.

Churchill was bewildered and saddened by the election results. It was painfully clear to him that the British people wished to make a complete break with the past. Much of his later writing about this period in his life evinces extreme bitterness. In one passage he wrote of the power he had held "for five years and three months of world war, at the end of which time, all our enemies having surrendered unconditionally or being about to do so, I was immediately dismissed by the British electorate from all further conduct of their affairs." After their years of suffering, most Britons wanted new, radical programmes to repair the damage done by the war. They favoured the Labour government's proposals for the socialization of medicine—the establishing of a system of free health care. Labour had also promised

The Dark Ages may return—the Stone Age may return on the gleaming wings of science; and what might now shower immeasurable material blessings upon mankind may even bring about its total destruction.
—WINSTON CHURCHILL speaking at Fulton, Missouri, on March 5, 1946

Clement R. Attlee (1883–1967) and Winston Churchill, his predecessor as prime minister, were a study in contrasts, and neither man's opinion of the other was high. When asked what Churchill really did in the war, Attlee said, "Talk about it." Churchill called Attlee "a modest man with much to be modest about."

Winston Churchill was deeply distressed by his defeat at the polls in 1945, but Clementine Churchill, who hoped her husband would retire, was relieved. "It may well be a blessing in disguise," she told him. "At the moment," he said, "it seems quite effectively disguised."

Churchill took up painting as a relief from tension during World War I. An increasingly enthusiastic amateur, he was particularly fond of the brilliant colours he found in southern France. He once said that he planned to spend his first million years in heaven learning to paint well—but only in bright colours.

to look beyond merely replacing war-damaged homes. They intended to institute a new housing policy that would banish slums from the face of Britain forever. Churchill had never made promises like these. For most people Churchill represented a world that had had its heyday. The general feeling was that Churchill and the members of his own class had known their century of glory, and the ordinary people wanted a kind of society that Churchill could never have approved.

Despite this rejection he had more energy than ever. As the senior member of the Conservative party, he made many speeches attacking the policies of the Labour government. The ways of these new politicians angered him. Churchill felt that the Labourite vision of a socialistic, welfare-oriented state smacked of communism—a system that he had always loathed.

These were not glorious times for Churchill. The war had ended, and the world was a different place.

He was out of touch with the mood of his countrymen. During the election campaign he had accused Labour of working to turn Britain into a totalitarian state. In one radio broadcast he declared that "There can be no doubt that Socialism is inseparably interwoven with totalitarianism and the abject worship of the State. . . . Socialism is in its essence an attack not only upon British enterprise, but upon the right of an ordinary man or woman to breathe freely without having a harsh, clumsy, tyrannical hand clapped across their mouth and nostrils. A free Parliament—look at that—a free Parliament is odious to the Socialist doctrinaire."

The fact that Clement Attlee and his colleagues were only hoping to correct the injustices that Churchill and Lloyd George had fought against for a brief period just a few decades earlier no longer mattered to Churchill. This new breed of British politician had made the mistake, in Churchill's

New York City greeted Churchill in 1946 with London-style weather, protective policemen, and vast crowds of cheering admirers. The former prime minister was en route to Fulton, Missouri, where 40,000 people—including President Truman—heard him deliver the speech in which he declared that due to Soviet expansionism an "iron curtain [had] descended across the continent of Europe."

Churchill's animosity towards the Soviet Union inspired reciprocal feelings among his former allies. This 1948 Soviet propaganda poster shows the Red Army confronting Churchill and a band of capitalistic "warmongers" across the ruins of Hitler's Third Reich. The caption bids the Western "firebugs" to "remember the dishonourable end of their predecessors."

> *For my part, I consider that it will be found much better by all parties to leave the past to history, especially as I propose to write that history myself.*
> —WINSTON CHURCHILL speaking in the House of Commons on January 23, 1948

view, of seeking total reform. Their egalitarian emphasis upon making the first moves toward a redistribution of wealth dismayed him.

The differences between Churchill's Conservatives and Attlee's Labourites became dramatically apparent at the opening of the new Parliament on August 1, 1945. One of the 189 remaining Conservatives gazed at the ranks of the Labour members—all 393 of them—and remarked, "Gracious, they look just like our constituents."

When Churchill entered the chamber, the Conservatives greeted him with a stirring rendition of "For He's a Jolly Good Fellow." The Labourites promptly rose to their feet and hit back with the communist anthem entitled "The Red Flag."

To exercise his creative spirit, Churchill began seriously to cultivate his longtime interest in painting. He also started to devote much of his time to writing *The Second World War,* a huge work in six volumes. Describing the many great battles in painstaking detail, he conveyed all the drama of war and also offered an elegant defence of his military strategies, which had begun to draw a measure of criticism.

Churchill remained immensely active during the five years from 1946 to 1951. Nothing could dampen his zeal for the challenge of political life—not even age or declining health. Wishing to be considered an elder statesman, he began to speak in public more frequently. In March 1946 he delivered a speech at Fulton, Missouri, in which he warned his audience that the ideological conflict between Soviet communism and the Western capitalist democracies could erupt into a third world war if relations were not improved. This particular speech made the headlines immediately. Churchill had become convinced that America's leaders were mistaken in assuming that the ideals of the Grand Alliance (between Britain, the United States and the Soviet Union) could be expected to survive into peacetime. He criticized the Americans for hoping that the newly established United Nations organization would prove to be the key to international cooperation.

Churchill's words changed the nature of Anglo-Soviet relations and conjured up a vision of the postwar world that many American diplomats did not share until 1947, by which time it had become apparent that the Soviet Union had no intention of allowing free elections in the eastern European countries that it had occupied since 1945.

The speech that Churchill made at Fulton was powerful and uncompromising: "Nobody knows what Soviet Russia and its Communist international organization intends to do in the near future, or what are the limits, if any, to their expansive and proselytizing tendencies. . . . From Stettin in the Baltic to Trieste in the Adriatic an iron curtain has descended across the Continent. . . . I do not believe that Soviet Russia desires war. What they desire is the fruits of war and the indefinite expansion of their power and doctrines." Churchill re-

Former *Luftwaffe* commander Hermann Göring in a pensive mood in between hearings at the trial of the Nazi leadership for war crimes in 1946. Göring, the most defiant of the 22 major defendants, cheated his would-be executioners by taking poison shortly before he was scheduled to hang.

> *How can one work up an intense dislike for a man who has 'borne the heat and burden of the day,' whose abilities are unquestionable, even though directed into the wrong channels, and who concentrates in his person such varied and brilliant qualities?*
> —EMMANUEL SHINWELL
> Labor party M.P.

peatedly stressed that the game of international politics was much deadlier than ever before, now that the world was living in the shadow of the atomic bomb. Many people found Churchill's comments valuable and Churchill took it upon himself to attend the first meeting of the Council of Europe in 1949. His opponents, however, sometimes felt that he was seeking the formation of a Western bloc intended to confront the Soviet Union. One newspaper suggested that Churchill was "not seeking a United Europe, but a Divided Europe." On the home front, Churchill continued to speak out against the government's policy of nationalization.

In February 1950 national elections were held and Churchill ran as his party's candidate for prime minister. Even though he had the backing of the Conservative party and spoke wisely about the dangers of an arms race with the Soviets, he lost the election. However, he was not ready to admit defeat. The Labour majority had been cut drasti-

Election day, 1950. Churchill campaigned hard, announcing his intention of restoring Britain to her "true place . . . at the head of an empire on which the sun never sets." He even responded humorously to gibes about his age with a formal denial that he was dead. The Conservatives lost anyway, but by only six seats.

Nuremberg was one of many German cities heavily damaged by bombs during World War II. In his postwar speeches Churchill emphasized the far more extensive devastation wrought by the atomic bomb in Hiroshima.

cally, and it was obvious that another election would be fought very soon. In 1951, at the age of 77, Churchill led his party into electoral fray once again. It was a time of economic difficulty in Britain, and social unrest was widespread. Churchill accused the Labour government of having failed to deliver on its promises.

In a moment of great personal triumph, Churchill won the election. Yet as soon as he took office as prime minister, he realized the true extent of the problems that had beset the previous administration. He also found that Conservative policies were no antidote to the nation's difficulties. The Attlee government had done an excellent job of rebuilding the country after the war. But the unexpected crisis of the Korean War (which had broken out in 1950) had forced the government to increase defence spending to the detriment of social programmes. The British people were not at all happy at being asked to make cutbacks.

As always, the grand arena of foreign affairs attracted Churchill more than the often undignified dogfight of domestic politics. He constantly ad-

> *There can hardly ever have been a war more easy to prevent than this second Armageddon.... Britain, France, and the United States have only to repeat the same well-meaning, short-sighted behaviour towards the new problems which in singular resemblance confront us today to bring about a third convulsion from which none may live to tell the tale.*
> —WINSTON CHURCHILL
> in his *The Gathering Storm*, 1948

dressed the issue of world peace and felt obliged to play a part in its preservation. Churchill had long believed that the way to handle world affairs was through high-level summit meetings, and in 1952 he went to Washington to meet with President Truman. He was received warmly in the United States, but the days were gone when a British prime minister could consider himself to be on an equal footing with an American president. Britain was now, to some extent, reduced to the status of a spectator at the game of international power politics.

The years of Churchill's postwar term as prime minister were not nearly as glamorous as those in which he had wielded immense imperial power against a backdrop of global conflagration. In the end, Churchill pursued much the same foreign policy as had the previous government. After the death of Stalin in 1953, Churchill became aware of both the need for change and the advisability of conducting a cautious retreat from his tendency towards instinctive anticommunism. He began to relax his attitude towards the Soviets. Just as he had worked to welcome Germany back into the commu-

After the costly, three-year-long Korean War ended with an armistice in 1953, Churchill voiced the hopes of most Britons. "When the advance of destructive weapons enables everyone to kill everybody else," he said in a speech to Parliament, "nobody will want to kill anybody at all."

After receiving the Order of the Garter from Queen Elizabeth II (b. 1926), Churchill was known as Sir Winston. He proudly wore his new regalia, complete with cloak, plumed hat, and decorations, to Elizabeth's coronation in June 1953.

nity of nations after the war, Churchill was now prepared to establish a more constructive relationship with the Soviet Union.

The Winston Churchill who was prime minister in the early 1950s was not the formidable figure that people remembered from an earlier period. He had aged, his step had slowed, and he had lost some of his once-legendary mental energy. Many people now believed he was too old for high public office. Despite all this, he gained increasing recognition for his lifetime of service. In 1953 Churchill received two great honours: he was knighted by the young Queen Elizabeth II, and he was awarded the Nobel Prize for Literature in honour of his fabulous mastery of the English language.

The strain of office had begun to wear on Churchill; increasingly anxious about his health, he consulted his doctor every day. In 1953 he suffered a stroke and was forced to abandon plans for a new summit meeting. Although he managed to travel to

> *I have never accepted what many... have kindly said, namely that I inspired the nation.... It was the nation and the race dwelling all round the globe that had the lion's heart.*
> —WINSTON CHURCHILL
> receiving the nation's tribute on his 80th birthday

> *There have been, no doubt, debaters and orators of equal resource and power, but few with that gift of puckish and rather mischievous humour which so endears [Churchill] to us.*
> —HAROLD MACMILLAN
> leading Conservative, speaking in the House of Commons, July 28, 1964

Washington early in 1954 to meet with President Eisenhower, the trip severely taxed his failing strength. Advancing age had not, however, impaired either his ready wit or his capacity for hitting back at political opponents with a few well-chosen words.

On November 30, 1954, Churchill turned 80 years old. During the greater part of those 80 years he had made a remarkable number of friends and enemies in politics; and yet he always retained an ability to feel affection toward even his fiercest opponents. He preferred opponents who were sincere in their beliefs to allies who lacked the courage of their convictions. On the occasion of his birthday, his friends and colleagues paid tribute to him at a huge ceremony in the Houses of Parliament. It was then that he knew the time had come for him to step down.

Churchill hung on until he was certain that his party's position was secure, and finally resigned as prime minister in April 1955. Anthony Eden, who had been not only his loyal foreign secretary both during the war and since 1951, but also the first senior politician to heed Churchill's warnings about Hitler, became his successor.

At the end of his career in high public office, Winston Churchill received the accolade of his own countrymen and the recognition and respect of many people around the world. Even after he retired as prime minister, he stayed on in Parliament until 1959. He also published yet another book, *A History of the English-Speaking Peoples*. This, his tenth major work, filled four volumes and is a monument to Churchill's love of tradition and the pride he took in being English.

Before his life ended, Churchill was to receive still more honours. Churchill College of Cambridge University was built and named for him. Another came in 1963, when he was made an honorary citizen of the United States. Churchill had always felt a special bond with America, and it was often suggested that he inherited his ebullient and outspoken manner from his American grandfather.

When Churchill died in 1965 at the age of 90, he

received a state funeral—a privilege normally reserved for the monarch. This was an honour without precedent for an Englishman not of the royal blood. Thousands of people from all around the world came to pay tribute to one of Britain's most faithful servants, the man who had promised his countrymen nothing but "blood, toil, tears, and sweat" in 1940 and had led them to a victory built on the foundations of patriotic self-sacrifice. He was buried near his parents in the small village of Bladon, not far from his birthplace at Blenheim Palace. In the great halls of Westminster Abbey was placed a stone that said "Remember Winston Churchill."

Churchill's countrymen have not forgotten him. During his 60 years of public office, the decisions of this man whom American historian William Manchester called "the Last Lion" often determined the fate of hundreds of thousands of people beyond the borders of his native land, especially during World War II.

Churchill's judgment was not always as sound as one might have hoped, however, especially in matters of strategy. During World War II he often made life difficult for his senior field commanders, and one move in particular now stands out as an example of poor judgment. British soldiers remember to this day Winston's firing of General Claude Auchinleck in 1942. As commander in chief in the Middle East and North Africa, Auchinleck, a thoroughly competent general, was slowly, but cleverly, engineering a crushing victory in that theatre of operations. Yet he suffered disgrace because Churchill, wanting a quick win for propaganda purposes, acted out of haste and shortsightedness.

Still, though not entirely without flaws, Churchill's record of service justifies claims of genius. Much of his greatness resulted from his understanding of the power of language. He cultivated a mastery of this medium from his earliest adolescence. As a statesman, his speeches were some of the most inspiring ever written. He had a rare ability to speak with skill and conviction on matters of public policy; the Atlantic Charter and the call for nothing but total victory in World War II

> *His nature, identified with a magnificent enterprise, his countenance, etched by the fires and frosts of great events, had become inadequate to the era of mediocrity.*
> —CHARLES DE GAULLE
> French soldier and statesman, upon Churchill's defeat in 1945

Churchill's 1965 funeral. RAF fighters roared overhead, the strains of "Rule Britannia" filled the cold January air, and the Tower of London's guns thundered their farewell. After the service, the statesman's coffin was taken to Bladon churchyard, near Blenheim Palace, where he was buried beside his parents.

During the last years of his life, Churchill often talked of death, but the prospect held no fear for the old adventurer. "I'm ready to meet my maker," he said. "Whether my maker is prepared for the great ordeal of meeting me is another matter."

were as instrumental as bombs and bullets in building toward absolute triumph.

It has been said that a person of genius differs from ordinary people not in any innate quality of the brain but by reason of his aims, purposes, and conviction. This can certainly be said of Winston Churchill. Throughout his life he held the greatest of purposes—to play a leading part in the protection and preservation of the nation he so loved.

It has also been said that evidence of great aspirations can be seen in a person who possesses a capacity for intense concentration. Churchill's concentration gave him a clarity of mind that often allowed him to see all sides of an issue, and to set down his thoughts in writing with immense precision and skill.

Winston Churchill, though the grandson of an English duke, was in many ways a self-made man. Often quite unconcerned with what others thought of him, he spoke his mind freely and would let nothing stand between him and the realization of his visions. He was a man like no one else; a man whose dreams became realities. Sir Winston Churchill, twice prime minister, longtime Member of Parliament, orator, and historian, will undoubtedly be remembered as one of 20th-century Britain's greatest leaders.

Further Reading

Cannadine, David (Ed) *Blood, Toil, Tears and Sweat: Winston Churchill's Famous Speeches* Cassell 1989

Churchill, Randolph S *Winston S Churchill Vol. I: Youth 1874–1900* Heinemann 1966

Churchill, Randolph S *Winston S Churchill Vol. II: The Young Statesman 1901–1914* Heinemann 1967

Churchill, Sir Winston S *Boer War* Mandarin 1990

Gilbert, Martin *Winston S Churchill Vol. III: The Challenge of War 1914–16* Heinemann 1971

Gilbert, Martin *Winston S Churchill Vol. IV: The Prophet of Truth 1922–39* Heinemann 1977

Manchester, William *The Caged Lion: Winston Spencer Churchill 1932–40* Cardinal 1989

Chronology

Nov. 30, 1874	Born Winston Leonard Spencer Churchill at Blenheim Palace
1888	Enters Harrow School
Sept. 1, 1893	Enters Royal Military Academy, Sandhurst
Jan. 24, 1895	His father, Randolph Churchill, dies
1897	Churchill serves with Malakand Field Force in India
1898	Serves with Kitchener's army in the Sudan Publishes his first book, *The History of the Malakand Field Force*
Dec. 12, 1899	Escapes from Pretoria after being taken prisoner while covering Boer War for the London *Morning Post*
Oct. 1, 1990	Elected Conservative Member of Parliament for Oldham
May 1904	Joins the Liberal party
1905	Appointed Undersecretary of State for the Colonies
1908	Appointed president of the Board of Trade
Sept. 12, 1908	Marries Clementine Hozier
1910	Appointed Home Secretary
1911	Appointed First Lord of the Admiralty
1915	Resigns from the Admiralty following Gallipoli disaster
1922	Loses seat in Parliament
1924	Reelected to Parliament, appointed Chancellor of the Exchequer, and rejoins Conservative party
1932–38	Warns British government and people against Hitler and German rearmament
Sept. 3, 1939	Britain declares war on Germany Churchill appointed First Lord of the Admiralty
May 10, 1940	Appointed Prime Minister
Aug. 12, 1941	Signs Atlantic Charter agreement with U.S. President Roosevelt
Jan. 1943	Confers with Roosevelt at Casablanca
1945	Confers with Roosevelt and Stalin at Yalta
May 8, 1945	Announces end of European war
July, 1945	Confers with Truman and Stalin at Potsdam
July 26, 1945	Conservative party defeated in general election
Oct. 26, 1951	Returns to office as prime minister following Conservative election victory
April 24, 1953	Invested Knight of the Garter by Queen Elizabeth II
Oct. 1953	Awarded Nobel Prize for Literature
April 5, 1955	Resigns as prime minister
Jan. 24, 1965	Dies, aged 90, of natural causes, at his home in London

Index

Afrika Korps, 83
Alamein, Battle of, 80
Ali, Tariq, 92
Ardennes offensive, 84
Asquith, Herbert, 44, 55, 58, 59
Atlantic Charter, 79, 106
atom bomb, 91–93
Attlee, Clement, 95, 98
Auchinleck, Claude, 105
Baldwin, Stanley, 63, 64
Battle of Britain, 76, 77
Belgium, 48, 49, 52, 74
Bladon, 105
Blenheim Palace, 20, 35
Boer War, 13, 15, 29, 36–38
Botha, Louis, 36
Bradley, Omar, 82
Brighton, 23
British Expeditionary Force, 52
British Union of Fascists, 67
Brooke, Rupert, 57
Bruce, Victor Alexander, ninth earl of Elgin, 43
Cambrai, 59
Carden, Sackville, 55, 56
Casablanca Conference, 81, 85
Chamberlain, Joseph, 33, 35, 36, 41, 42
Chamberlain, Neville, 68–71, 73, 74
Churchill, Clementine, 42, 44, 95
Churchill, Jack, 20, 22, 24, 28
Churchill, Jennie, 18, 21, 22, 28, 29
Churchill, John, first duke of Marlborough, 66
Churchill, Randolph, 19, 21–25, 27–29
Churchill, Winston, 8
    birth, 18, 20
    chancellor of the duchy of Lancaster, 58
    Chancellor of the Exchequer, 63, 64
    childhood, 19–25
    death, 20, 104, 106, 107
    education, 13, 19–28
    First Lord of the Admiralty, 47, 48–49, 51–58, 71
    Home Secretary, 45, 46–47
    knighthood, 20, 103
    literary career, 13, 28, 30–36, 63, 65–66, 99, 103, 104
    marriage, 42, 44
    military career, 27, 29–35, 58
    minister of munitions, 59
    president of the Board of Trade, 44–46
    Prime Minister, 74–77, 79–82, 84–90, 91, 101–104
    secretary of state for the colonies, 61
    secretary of state for war and air, 60
    under-secretary of state for the colonies, 43–44
Churchill College, 104
Conservative party, 32, 34, 35, 41–43, 63, 64, 90, 95, 97, 98, 100
Contasini, Mario, 8
Cuba, 30
Czechoslovakia, 68, 70
Daily Graphic, 30
Daily Telegraph, 32
Daladier, Edouard, 69
Dardanelles campaign, 53–57
D-Day, 82
de Gaulle, Charles, 83
de Tocqueville, Alexis, 9, 11
Democracy in America, 9
Denmark, 73
Dunkirk, 75, 77
Durban, 9, 38
Eden, Anthony, 104
Edward VII, king, 46
Edward VIII, king, 67
Eisenhower, Dwight D., 80, 82, 83, 86, 87, 104
Elgin, Lord *see* Bruce, Victor Alexander, ninth earl of Elgin
Elizabeth II, queen, 103
Emerson, Ralph Waldo, 10, 11
England *see* Great Britain
Enola Gay, 92, 93
Estcourt, 36, 38
Everest, Elizabeth, 13, 22
Federalist Papers, 10
Fisher, John, first baron Fisher of Kilverstone, 47, 48
Fourth Hussars, 27
France, 54, 73, 75–77, 86, 87
Franco, Francisco, 77
Franz Ferdinand, archduke of Austria, 49
Free French, 83

Führerprinzip, 9
Gallipoli, 55, 56
Gandhi, Mohandas K., 66
Gascoyne-Cecil, Robert, third marquis of
    Salisbury, 33
George V, king of Great Britain, 46, 67
George VI, king of Great Britain, 67
Germany, 47–53, 55–57, 67–71, 73–86, 88
Göring, Hermann, 78, 97
Great Britain,
    domestic policy, 45–47, 48, 64–65, 96–97
    foreign policy, 16, 35, 43, 47, 49, 59–61,
        69–71, 79, 82, 88, 89, 99
    World War I and, 19, 29, 49, 51–59
    World War II and, 19, 20, 71, 73–88, 105,
        106
Hamilton, Alexander, 10
Harrow School, 23, 25
Hiroshima, 90, 92, 93
History of the English-Speaking Peoples, A,
    104
Hitler, Adolf, 8, 68–71, 78–86, 87, 88
Hozier, Clementine *see* Churchill, Clementine
India, 31, 32, 33, 64, 65
Ireland, 60, 61
Italy, 81
James, William, 8
Japan, 80, 84, 87, 88, 90–93
Jerome, Leonard, 21
Jews, 69, 71
King, Ernest, 85
Kitchener, Horatio Herbert, 29, 32, 33, 34, 51
Korea, 101, 102
Labour party, 63, 90, 93, 95, 98, 101
Ladysmith, Battle of, 39
Leahy, William D., 92
Lend-Lease Bill, 78–79
Lenin, Vladimir, 8
Liberal party, 35, 42–47, 63
Lincoln, Abraham, 11
Lloyd George, David, 43, 45, 48, 52, 59, 61, 63
Luftwaffe, 77, 78, 99
Luxembourg, 73
Maginot Line, 74
Mahdi, 34
Marlborough, 66

Marxism, 7, 8
Mers-el-Kebir, 76
Miami, Florida, 8
Morning Post, The, 32, 33, 36, 37
Morning Star, The, 13
Mosley, Oswald, 67
Munich, 8, 70
Mussolini, Benito, 69, 70
Nagasaki, 90
Natal, 36, 39
National Socialist German Workers' party,
    67–71, 74, 75, 78, 82
Nazi party *see* National Socialist German
    Workers' party
Netherlands, the, 73
New York City, 8
Niebuhr, Reinhold, 10
Nobel Prize for Literature, 103
Normandy, 82, 86, 87
North Africa, 80
Norway, 73
Nuremberg, 101
Oldham, 35, 41
Omdurman, Battle of, 33, 34
Operation Overlord, 82, 87
Order of the Garter, 103
Parliament, 31, 41–47, 63–65, 75, 90
Patton, George, 83
Pearl Harbour, Hawaii, 80, 84
Pétain, Henri Philippe, 70, 83
Poland, 70, 71
Potsdam Conference, 88, 89, 91
Rhodes, Cecil, 16
River War, The, 35
Romania, 57
Rommel, Erwin, 79, 83
Roosevelt, Franklin Delano, 8, 78, 79, 81, 85,
    86, 87, 88
Royal Air Force, 19, 76–79
Royal Military Academy, Sandhurst, 24, 25,
    27, 28, 29
Royal Navy, 47, 48–49, 54–55, 77, 79
Russian Revolution, 60
Salisbury, Lord *see* Gascoyne-Cecil, Robert,
    third marquis of Salisbury

Sandhurst *see* Royal Military Academy, Sandhurst
Second World War, The, 99
Shaw, George Bernard, 67
Sidney Street, London, 46
Simpson, Wallis Warfield, 67
South Africa, 13, 30, 34–39, 43
Soviet Union *see* Union of Soviet Socialist Republics
Spanish-American War, 29
Spanish Civil War, 77
Stalin, Joseph, 19, 80, 85–88, 93, 102
Story of the Malakand Field Force, The, 32
Sudan, the, 32, 33, 34
tanks, 59
Tolstoy, Leo, 7
Transvaal, 30, 35, 37, 44
Truman, Harry, 88, 89, 90, 91, 102
Turkey, 53–56

U-boats, 55, 79
Union of Soviet Socialist Republics, 60, 61, 68, 70, 71, 79, 86, 87, 97, 98, 100, 102, 103
United States, 41, 79, 80, 99, 104
Victoria, queen, 31, 34, 55
Warsaw, 71
von Bethmann-Hollweg, Theobald, 49
War and Peace, 7
White, George, 36, 39
Wilson, Woodrow, 8
women's suffrage, 41
World Crisis, The, 66
World War I, 49–60
    see also Great Britain, World War I and
World War II, 73–89
    see also Great Britain, World War II and,
Yalta Conference, 85–86, 88
Zangara, Giuseppe, 8